THOMISM AND TOLERANCE

THOMISM AND TOLERANCE

JOHN F. X. KNASAS

University of Scranton Press
Scranton and London

Library of Congress Cataloging-in-Publication Data

Knasas, John F. X.
  Thomism and tolerance / John F.X. Knasas.
     p. cm.
  Includes bibliographical references (p.   ) and index.
  ISBN 978-1-58966-215-5 (cloth)
  1. Toleration. 2. Thomas, Aquinas, Saint, 1225?-1274. I. Title.
  BJ1431.K63 2010
  179'.9--dc22

                                                    2010044691

Distribution:
University of Scranton Press
Chicago Distribution Center
11030 S. Langley
Chicago, IL 60628

PRINTED IN THE UNITED STATES OF AMERICA

FOR J. M.

CONTENTS

INTRODUCTION

In 2003, I published *Being and Some Twentieth-Century Thomists*. Its theme is a philosophical assessment of the last century's great revival of interest in the philosophy of St. Thomas Aquinas. My reflection uncovered the notion of being (*ratio entis*) as a common object of interest among Thomists. Debates swirled around whether being was *a posteriori* or *a priori* and around how to basically describe the notion. Some said that to be a being means to be a possessor of Aristotelian form; others, without denying a role for form, insisted that the decisive addition was the act of existing (*actus essendi* or *esse*).

What surprised me, however, was discovering how central the notion of being is for Aquinas' ethical thinking. In my discussion of the varied Thomistic opinions about the self-evidency of the first principle of morality—the good ought to be done—I realized that the subject of the proposition is again the notion of being. Since being does not make complete abstraction from its differences, being is apprehended as a concrescence of perfection and merits the denomination of "the good." But the subject of the first moral principle is not being, bare and simple. More precisely, it is being as understood and intellected by the human. This thinking presents the human as a particularly intense presencing of being among all the other instances of being. Before the human instance understood in this way, we are not necessitated or constrained as the human will's first motion is necessitated when intellectually presented with the good. Neither are we left totally free as we are before any particular instance of the good. Rather, the object here provokes another reaction. Before the human as a particularly intense presencing of the good through the human's intellection of being, we understand an obligation to exercise our freedom in a respectful and solicitous manner. We apprehend a call to love.

Thomism and Tolerance continues this line of thinking. What are the implications of looking at our fellows as intellectors of being? What should human behavior be like to be congruent with this fact which, for Aquinas, is true even if we deny it or do not recognize it? For despite the

1

refined and academic nature of Aquinas' discussion of the notion of being, his discussion is more akin to depth psychology. We do not have to wait until we study Aquinas to learn the notion of being. The notion of being is such an automatic abstraction of the intellect that it can lie unnoticed in our lives but nevertheless have conscious effects.

As I explain in chapters II and III, being controls—and has always controlled—human psychology. Though not the entire story, the intellection of being is the central philosophical theme about the human. The intellection of being is there when we are moral; it is there when we are immoral. It is there when we understand, and it is there when we do not understand. Such thinking obviously opens our lives to others. For, as discordant as philosophies are, a commensurating psychology exists. No matter how erroneous my interlocutor is, even no matter how vicious my interlocutor is, my interlocutor cannot efface the intellection of being within himself. Being's indelible presence continues to call for my respect and for my efforts to find common ground.

In chapter V, I attempt to practice what I preach by analyzing the major ethical traditions of hedonism, utilitarianism, and Kantianism in light of Aquinas' philosophical psychology. I also attempt to engage the political and social thinking of John Rawls and Richard Rorty. Chapter VI attempts to do the same in respect to the sweep of cultural history as described by Christopher Dawson. In my opinion, Dawson's narrative is an antidote to Nietzsche's genealogy of morals. Nietzsche's philological analysis of ancient moral terms in which "good" means strong and "bad" means weak is simply too parochial.

Aquinas' engaged and respective stance to our fellows is the entry to topics of tolerance. The stance impacts upon the way dialogue should be initiated and conducted, legislation should be enacted, artistic creativity should be exercised, and different cultures should be appreciated. Aquinas' approach from his philosophical psychology will strike some as too naive and too intellectual. In Aquinas' defense, the charge of naivety is too simplistic. As I will recount in chapter II, Aquinas knew well the intellector of being's resources for willful malice—the passions and our default position of nonconsideration of the rule. Moreover, Aquinas was no pacifist. Both individuals and the state can exercise self-defense, though only in qualified circumstances.

Nevertheless, Aquinas never gave up on knowledge having an effect. For example, the number of angels that remained firm was greater than those who sinned. Also, human beings are not so sunk in sin that they cannot, little by little, be led back to virtue by reason. Finally, we have Aquinas' own example. I know of few if any philosophical issues that Aquinas resolved by recourse to nonphilosophical (or political) means. He dealt with his opponents by expending himself in intellectual discourse. Not surprisingly then, the opening pages of *Aeterni patris* (Pope Leo XIII's 1878 encyclical enjoining a return to study of the thought of Aquinas) introduce the recommendation of Aquinas with this explanation: "But the natural helps with which the grace of divine wisdom, strongly and sweetly disposing all things, has supplied the human race are neither to be despised nor neglected, chief among which is evidently the right use of philosophy. For not in vain did God set the light of reason in the human mind." My conclusion is that Aquinas' realistic attitude—yet his continued commitment to reason—make an investigation of his philosophical psychology all the more imperative. What can Aquinas be contemplating to justify his fundamental commitment to reason despite frank acknowledgments of human irrationality? Is his commitment just an expression of a manic moment or the result of something truly objective?

I gave the backbone of the following chapters as a series of eight lectures at the Kaunas Technological University in Kaunas, Lithuania, during Spring 2004, U.S. Fulbright grant. The lectures were entitled, "Lessons on Truth and Tolerance from the Christian Middle Ages." I deeply appreciate the invitation of Dr. Lina Šulcienė of KTU to participate in the lecture series. But most of all, I thank Dr. Šulcienė for the opportunity to push my understanding of Aquinas' metaphysics to that of a psychology living throughout the histories of human societies.

I

IS TRUTH INCOMPATIBLE WITH TOLERANCE?

1. The Ideal of Tolerance

This book's title, *Thomism and Tolerance*, may sound like a historical contradiction. For when one thinks of Thomism, one thinks of Aquinas, and when one thinks of Aquinas, one thinks of the Christian Middle Ages—and so, the Crusades, the Christian mistreatment of the Jews, and the Spanish Inquisition. In light of these events, the Christian Middle Ages seem intolerant. Hence, how could Thomism go along with tolerance?

No doubt, various strategies exist to dispute the intolerance charge as it is based on the above events. For example, the Crusades were not originally intended to impose the Christian religion on the Muslims but to protect Christians from the imposition of Islam. Also, Christians believed the Jews were in fact subversive, and being tolerant certainly does not mean that you cannot defend yourself. Finally, the Spanish Inquisition was an affair chiefly run by secular rulers and not by the Church. But my intention is not to debate these strategies. My focus is not on facts but on ideas and what I see to be their logical implications. And so I admit that people acting from my (to be described) principles of tolerance could also be victims of erroneous judgments of fact that cast their fellows as recalcitrant opponents. That tragedy is always a possibility. Here I will only say that, in my position, the victim does not have to be so respectful that the victim cannot ethically defend himself against the de facto intolerant.

My thesis is that Aquinas' natural law ethics grounds the ideal of tolerance that is so treasured in current Western democracies better than other ethical traditions. I acknowledge that tolerance is an indispensable portion of the common good, the good that belongs properly to society itself. Moreover, tolerance expresses something that any philosophy that claims to be adequate must accommodate and make sense of. Gone are the days when a philosopher could philosophize in splendid isolation from society and without any regard to the social implication of his ideas. No, every philosopher must be held to the test of accommodating—even grounding —this undeniable aspect of the common good that is tolerance. That test is as important for good philosophy as is following the laws of logic. Not only must the Thomist pass this test, so must the hedonist, the utilitarian, the Marxist, the Kantian, and so on.

I also want to insist that the word *tolerance*, as it is usually understood, is actually too weak to express the social good about which I am talking. Usually, tolerance suggests that though I disagree with you, I simply do nothing to hurt you. If you have ever been part of a backbiting community, then you know that this minimal sense of tolerance is no mean thing. But like John Locke,[1] I want to speak about tolerance not just as mutual indifference but also as mutual assistance. In speaking of tolerance, then, I do not want to limit myself to mutual indifference. I do not just want to exist with others but to live with others. In this more robust sense of tolerance, our fellows stand ready to help. And so one can presume on the part of others a goodwill that does not automatically cast one's words and actions in a suspicious light and does not strive to find "the fly in the ointment" of what one says.

In short, "brotherly tolerance" or "fraternal tolerance" expresses better this undeniable component of the common good. No human ever ostracizes another. The lines of communication not only remain open; they remain active. In fact, one can claim that this component is more important to the common good than material things—fine buildings, hospitals, roads, a power and sanitation system, and culture—for from mutual concern these others will follow. This ideal of tolerance works from the assumption that our fellows are acting, or are capable of acting, from the best motives of conscience in coming to their decisions about the ultimate nature of reality and about appropriate human behavior.[2]

A reader might wonder if in widening tolerance from mutual indifference to mutual assistance I have equivocated on the meaning of tolerance. One might say that my wider sense is not tolerance at all but something else. For instance, the wider sense is fraternity. Fraternity includes the narrower sense of tolerance and sustains it, but fraternity is not itself tolerance. Consequently, my title should be *Thomsim and Fraternity*. Similarly, Michael Walzer wonders if "enthusiastic endorsement of difference" ought to be placed on the continuum of attitudes called tolerant. He pointedly asks, "But perhaps this last attitude falls outside my subject: how can I be said to tolerate what I in fact endorse?"[3] My sense of tolerance appears to be too *pro* otherness and not enough *con*.

Prima facie, this remark is sensible. But further reflection observes that the remark misses a tertium quid. The mental landscape includes more than mutual indifference and fraternity. Mutual indifference is tolerance outside of a context of fraternity. There is something that is tolerance within that context. Fraternity is not simply a *pro*-attitude to all difference; it still involves a nonapproval but acceptance of difference that is central to the idea of tolerance. But fraternal tolerance is markedly unlike mutual-indifference tolerance. The latter accepts logically, or at least de facto, unbridgeable chasms between oneself and "the other." One is left to withdraw into one's group, if incommensurability has not destroyed that.[4] Society becomes impossible—or possible only for fleeting reasons that still do not address a growing feeling of alienation. Also, mutual-indifference tolerance leads to a lack of interest in the other that breeds an ignorance of the other and plants the seeds of future misunderstandings and conflicts. In contrast, fraternal tolerance contains the view that beneath all difference exists a sameness that grounds a respect, which subsequent difference or otherness cannot obliterate. Again, no one ever is written off.

I will argue that in Aquinas' natural law ethics is a psychology of the intellector of being. This psychology is pervasive. It is there when one is moral; it is there when one is immoral. It is there when one is philosophically correct and when one is incorrect. Even anthropology à la Christopher Dawson will illustrate that this psychology is operative throughout cultural history. In sum, a whole need not destroy its parts. It can metamorphosize them. Fraternity is a whole that includes tolerance. But unlike the tolerance of mutual indifference, fraternal tolerance, while it fails to approve, is impelled to be engaged, respectful, and sympathetic of the other. It provides a powerful motivation for living one's life in fellowship—not in mutual indifference.

2. The Philosophical Problem of Truth and Tolerance

I wish to argue the thesis that Aquinas' natural law logically accommodates tolerance by countering the thesis that truth is an enemy of tolerance. In the West, the ideal of tolerance has gained in popularity from the realization that the cataclysms of the last century were caused by people who believed that their way was the only true way. In sum, the idea of the truth was the problem. So, if you thought that you knew the truth, you turn out to be the most socially dangerous of individuals. As American postmodernist Richard Rorty says, proponents of a commensurating discourse are, socially speaking, proponents of intolerance: "A 'mainstream' Western philosopher typically says: Now that such-and-such a line of inquiry has had such a stunning success, let us reshape all inquiry, and all of culture, on its model, thereby permitting objectivity and rationality to prevail in areas previously obscured by convention, superstition, and the lack of a proper epistemological understanding of man's ability to accurately represent nature."[5]

With this diagnosis, people saw skepticism as the cure for the disease. Hence, Rorty also says, "The compromise advocated in this book amounts to saying: *Privatize* the Nietzschean-Sartrean-Foucauldian attempt at authenticity and purity, in order to prevent yourself from slipping into a political attitude which will lead you to think that there is some social goal more important than avoiding cruelty."[6] Though Rorty says "privatize," he means "skepticize." There is no truth with a "T." For Rorty, reality is too indeterminate to privilege any philosophical discourse. Consequently, "anything could be made to look good or bad, important or unimportant, useful or useless, by being redescribed."[7] We will all get along if we all realize that no one can claim to possess the truth. As Rorty says, "To see one's language, one's conscience, one's morality, and one's highest hopes as contingent products, as literalizations of what once were accidentally produced metaphors, is to adopt a self-identity what suits one for citizenship in such an ideally liberal state. That is why the ideal citizen of such an ideal state would be someone who thinks of the founders and the preservers of her society as such poets, rather than as people who had discovered or who clearly envisioned the truth about the world or about humanity."[8]

But in fact, skepticism has not been a refuge. The failure to achieve an intellectual grounding was Frederick Nietzsche's cue to trumpet the will to power. This nineteenth-century German philosopher invited the strong to be themselves over the weak. In sections VII, X, and XII of the first essay in his *The Genealogy of Morals*, Nietzsche dissipated the spell of the weak that the strong are responsible for their actions and incurred "guilt" that only the Christian religion can remove. But the Nazis took inspiration from Nietzsche's voluntarism.[9] So the task of establishing a respect for tolerance is not as simple as the offer of skepticism. In fact, Rorty is aware that his position may not check the powerful—"the tendencies to cruelty inherent in searches for autonomy."[10] In chapter V, I investigate the success of Rorty's solution.

Another weakness in the skepticism defense is that skepticism could drive people into inhuman dogmatisms as happened with people attracted by Hegel-inspired Marxist philosophy. Etienne Gilson, a twentieth-century French Thomist and pioneering historian of medieval philosophy, sums up the second weakness: "Against the crude, yet fundamentally sound craving of Marxism for positive and dogmatic truth, the skepticism of our decadent philosophy has not a chance. It deserves to be destroyed as it actually is in the minds of many among our contemporaries who embrace Marxism because it is the only dogmatism they know. Not something less rational, or less constructive, but something more rational and more comprehensively constructive is required to meet its challenge."[11]

Basically—and contra Rorty—I want to take up Gilson's suggestion that democracy needs something that is more rational than skepticism and yet is not destructive of the democratic virtue of tolerance. That skepticism actually threatens democratic societies is an invitation to me to reassess the charge that all proponents of truth are also enemies of tolerance. As mentioned, I want to argue that the truth of Aquinas' natural law ethics better establishes tolerance than any other major ethical tradition.

3. Why a Theologian, Thomas Aquinas?

Why am I turning to a theologian to handle the philosophical problem of truth and tolerance? Will not Aquinas' ideas be too sectarian to be of interest to nonbelievers? As understandable as these questions are, they rely upon a simplistic understanding of theology that is not true of Aquinas. As Aquinas makes clear in the opening article of his *Summa Theologiae*, his responsibility was to explain the content of divine revelation. But he understood that content to include two kinds of truth: truth accessible to natural reason (such as God's existence and uniqueness, spirituality, and even moral truths as found in the Ten Commandments) and truth inaccessible to natural reason (such as the Trinity of persons in God's one nature, Christ in the Eucharist, Christ as the Son of God). To be noted is that even naturally known truth is included in God's speaking to us. This is not redundant on God's part because, left to our own resources, we could attain truth only after a long time and with much error. So, to avoid the impropriety of humans returning God's revelation by addressing the sun, for example, God also tells us that he is an infinite spiritual being. Such a point is something we could have figured out on our own but in fact probably would not have.

Hence, since Aquinas' duty as a theologian is to explain revelation and God's revelation includes truths knowable by natural reason, then when—in the course of doing his theology—Aquinas explains natural truths, Aquinas is necessarily doing philosophy. Just as you cannot explain a mathematical truth without doing mathematics, you cannot explain a philosophical truth without doing philosophy. So, Thomistic theology cannot be only theology; at certain times it will also be philosophy. A philosopher can turn to Aquinas at those times Aquinas is philosophizing. Just because Aquinas is a theologian, it does not follow that the only things that he says are theological. Of course, whether Aquinas' philosophical explanations are good ones can only be known by scrutiny of them, as I will go on to do.

NOTES:

[1] In speaking of toleration, John Locke desired a more robust concept: "Nay, we must not content ourselves with the narrow measures of bare justice; charity, bounty, and liberality must be added to it. This [1] the Gospel enjoins, [2] this reason directs, and [3] this that natural fellowship we are born into requires of us." John Locke, *A Letter Concerning Toleration*, ed., Mario Montnori (The Hague: Martinus Nijhoff, 1963), 33. But Locke provides little philosophical justification for points [2] and [3]. The motive for society is simply protection of temporal goods, and society is not something into which we are born (p. 83).

[2] My understanding of the ideal of tolerance includes the idea of openness to respectful dialogue that holds the promise of mutual agreement about basic ideas—for example, those ideas of Aquinas that I will go on to explicate. In my opinion, then, my understanding of tolerance appears to differ from that of UNESCO's "Declaration of Principles on Tolerance" of November 16, 1995. The document comes close to the minimal "mutual indifference" sense of tolerance when it says, "[Tolerance] means that one is free to adhere to one's own convictions and accepts that others adhere to theirs. It means accepting the fact that human beings, naturally diverse in their appearance, situation, speech, behaviour and values, have the right to live in peace and to be as they are. It also means that one's views are not to be imposed on others" (para. 1.4).

[3] Michael Walzer, *On Toleration* (New Haven, CT: Yale University Press, 1997), 11.

[4] Ibid., 100–102, speaks of postmodernism creating two centrifugal forces. One force splits groups off a common center, the second splits individuals from groups. The threat here is a population of dispirited isolated individuals. Walzer eschews a philosophical solution for a sociological and political one. Government must somehow—for example, through tax exemptions, matching grants, subsidies, and entitlements—shore up cultural groups and local communities. Ibid., 106. As I will soon note, my approach will remain philosophical. I believe that a solution-in-depth is possible here.

[5] Richard Rorty, *Philosophy and the Mirror of Nature* (Princeton, NJ: Princeton University Press, 1980), 367. Also, "The danger of re-enchanting the world, from a Deweyan point of view, is that it might interfere with the development of what Rawls calls 'a social union of social unions,' some of which may be (and in Emerson's view, should be) very small indeed. For it is hard to be both enchanted with one version of the world and tolerant of all the others." Richard Rorty, "The Priority of Democracy to Philosophy" in *Objectivity,*

Relativism, and Truth (Cambridge: Cambridge University Press, 1991), 195. Likewise, Richard J. Bernstein writes, "[Today] there is a deep suspicion, hostility and ridicule of any aspiration to unity, reconciliation, harmony, totality, the whole, the one. There is widespread bias that these signifiers mask repression and violence; that there is an inevitable slippage from totality to totalitarianism and terror." "Metaphysics, Critique, and Utopia," *The Review of Metaphysics*, 42 (1988): 259.

[6] Richard Rorty, *Contingency, Irony, and Solidarity* (Cambridge: Cambridge University Press, 1989), 65.

[7] Ibid., 7.

[8] Ibid., 61.

[9] See William L. Shirer, *The Rise and Fall of the Third Reich* (New York: Simon and Schuster, 1960), 99–101. "[Nietzsche or Loyola] are crazy because the limits are set by what *we* can take seriously. This, in turn, is determined by our upbringing, our historical situation." Richard Rorty, "Priority of Democracy to Philosophy," 187–188. This remark sounds like a Nietzschean arguing with Nietzsche. All that Rorty can do is be grateful that Germany lost World War II. For an excellent similar critique of the tolerance views of Locke, Hume, Burke, Russell, Popper, and Oakeshott, see Thomas A. Russman, *A Prospectus for the Triumph of Realism* (Macon, GA: Mercer University Press, 1987), ch. 8.

[10] Richard Rorty, "Priority of Democracy to Philosophy," 144. For Rorty's comments about Lyotard's criticisms of democratic society, see Rorty, "Cosmopolitanism without Emancipation: A Response to Jean-François Lyotard" in *Objectivity, Relativism, and Truth*, p. 214.

[11] Etienne Gilson, *The Unity of Philosophical Experience* (New York: Charles Scribner's Sons, 1937), 294.

II
THE BASIS OF HUMAN DIGNITY

To understand how Aquinas' natural law ethics better grounds tolerance in the context of fraternity, one must first understand the basis for human dignity in Aquinas' ethics. Like the Greeks before him, Aquinas locates the basis for human dignity in our rationality. At *Summa Theologiae* I, 29, 3c, Aquinas famously remarks, "*Person* signifies what is most perfect in all nature—that is a subsistent individual of rational nature." But this common formula must be glossed for its power to be experienced.

Often, rationality is presented in terms of discursion, or syllogizing. So, as rational, we are logic machines annoyingly spinning out one argument after another. But this description is a caricature. In order to function, syllogisms require what logic calls middle terms. For example, in the syllogism:

(1) Tom is a man;
(2) man is mortal;
(3) hence, Tom is mortal,

the middle term is *man*. It connects Tom with what we know about human nature so that we can conclude something about Tom. Some middle terms and what we understand about them may themselves be conclusions of syllogisms. But this process cannot be repeated indefinitely. Ultimately, there are middle terms known not by syllogism but by intuition or contemplation—also called intellection. Aquinas explains that the word *intellectus* is appropriate, for *intellectus* derives from the words *intus* and *legere* which together mean to read into.[1] So, buried within the traditional understanding of the human as rational is the more profound understanding of the human as intellector. To understand the dignity of the human as rational, one must understand the dignity of the human as an intellector.

I want to illustrate the connection between human dignity and intellection by speaking about the first principle of practical reason. Aquinas discusses this principle in a famous text in his natural law ethics. The text is article 2, question 94, of the first part of the second part of his *Summa Theologiae*. Few have noticed that the first practical principle is a call to be respectful and solicitous of ourselves and others.[2] In short, the first practical principle is a call to love. Consequently, this text is especially relevant as a Thomistic basis for tolerance.

1. Aquinas' *Ratio Entis*, the Notion of Being

Aquinas presents "The good ought to be done and evil avoided" as a *per se notum* (self-evident) proposition that is the first principle of practical reason. By a *per se notum* proposition, Aquinas says that he means a proposition in which the meaning of the predicate is contained in the meaning of the subject. How does Aquinas understand *the good* so that the notion includes oughtness? By *the good* Aquinas also means the notion of being, the *ratio entis*, which the article mentions as the basis of the first principle of speculative reason—the principle of noncontradiction. It makes sense to call being the good because being is an eminently rich intelligibility. By *intelligibility* I mean a commonality that can be grasped in the particular things presented by sensation.

"Generic" commonalities lose some of the richness of the real because they abstract from the differences of particular things. For example, the commonality that we find in Tom, Dick, and Harry, and which we intend to express by the term *human*, does not include Tom's pale complexion, Dick's ruddy complexion, or Harry's dark complexion. This lack of inclusion of the complexions is required to keep human nature common to all three individuals. The notion of being does not behave exactly like a generic notion. If being did not also include the differences of the particular things from which it is taken, then these differences would be reduced to nonbeing and a real plurality of things would cease to exist.

At *De Veritate* XXI, 1c, Aquinas says that the differences of a generic intelligibility remain in the intelligibility *implicitly and potentially*. This characterization implies that, with the intelligibility of being, the differences remain *implicitly* but *actually* within the notion of being.[3] Accordingly, at *De Veritate* I, 1c, the differences of being do not add to being from the outside but are said to "express" a mode of being. In the twentieth century, a Thomist like Maritain can say, "Everything which divides [electrons and angels] from one another is the same being which I find in each of them—varied. I simply have to fix my attention on it to see that it is at once one and multiple."

Others, like Phelan and Owens, describe the intelligibility of being as a sameness-in-difference.[4] Sameness-in-difference they also call an analogous intelligibility, or an analogon; instances that harbor that analogon, they call analogates.[5] For my purpose, I note that as keeping the differences of things to itself, the notion of being as an analogon has an unparalleled richness. This richness will make understandable the denomination of being as the good.

Hence, humans have some idea of what the Scholastics called the absolutely infinite in contrast to the relatively infinite. The latter lacks nothing in a particular line. For example, a ribbon without ends is an infinite amount of ribbon. Yet it is still ribbon and as such lacking in many perfections. The absolutely infinite lacks no perfection, even no conceivable perfection and no degree thereof. The classical theist tradition has long used the absolutely infinite to characterize God. Hence, we have Anselm's that-than-which-no-greater-can-be-thought, the rationalists' actually infinite being, Kant's discussion of the *ens realissimum*, and Vatican I's "one, true, living God, infinite in intellect and will, and in every perfection."

Charles Hartshorne, a follower of Alfred North Whitehead, has criticized the understanding of God as absolutely infinite on the ground that some perfections are mutually exclusive. For example, something cannot have at the same time the perfections of being both red and green all over. But before this linking of the infinite with God, Aquinas linked the infinite with the notion of being. As Aquinas says, being is that into which we resolve all of our concepts and being is added to not by bringing in something from the outside but by "expressing" a mode of being. In the notion of being, the intellect discerns an intelligible source from which streams all perfections. Hartshorne's objection applies to the perfections as expressed. He is remarkably incognizant of the intelligible ground out of whose depths the perfections arise.

To apprehend being is to experience an earthquake in one's intellectual life. Thereafter, one is not the same. Everything becomes of interest because every thing in its uniqueness gives one another look at the *ratio entis*, whose treasure contains this difference—and who knows what else. The more different beings that one knows, the better one sees the sameness that contains them all. Nevertheless, one would be wrong to think that intellectual pursuit demands an explicit philosophical presentation of the

above. Aquinas understands being as such an automatic abstraction from
self-manifestly real things provided by sensation that the *ratio entis* can lie
unnoticed in the depths of our conscious life and nevertheless have conscious effects. Such thinking about being goes a long way to explain why
the noncontradiction principle (something cannot both be and not be at the
same time and in the same respect), which is about being, is self-evident
to all, even those who never thought about the *ratio entis*.

2. Other Witnesses to the Notion of Being

But the overarching commonality of being was not Aquinas' discovery. In the Middle Ages, others spoke of it, though under different
names and with different interpretations. Earlier in his book, *De Libero arbitrio*, Augustine seems to talk of the same when speaking of wisdom as
truth:

> Men claim they are enthralled when they embrace the beautiful
> bodies of their wives or even courtesans. Do we doubt we are
> happy in the arms of truth? Men with throats parched with thirst
> cry out with joy when they find an abundant spring of pure
> water, or, if famished, when they discover a splendid dinner or
> supper. Shall we deny the happiness that comes from being
> given the food and drink that is truth? . . . Of those who choose
> by the light of the sun what they wish to enjoy seeing, there are
> those who if they were endowed with stronger, more healthy, or
> vigorous eyes, would love to look at nothing better than the sun
> itself which sheds its light on all the other things that delight
> weaker eyes. So too a powerful and penetrating mind, having
> seen with certainty many unalterable truths, turns to truth itself
> wherein all is revealed, clinging to it as if forgetful of all else
> and enjoying in it everything at once. For whatever delights us
> in other truths, does so by reason of truth itself.[6]

Augustine's description of wisdom—as the enveloping context in
which we see the truths used to judge what we sense—presents wisdom as
a context by which human awareness appreciates things. Things do not appear in themselves but as over and against wisdom. As such, wisdom is a
mediating factor in human awareness. Moreover, in Augustine's interpretation, the light of truth is more like colored light rather than natural light.
In other words, the light of truth has content. As just quoted above, truth
has "everything at once." So, the light of truth appears to be a constitutive

a priori. Also, wisdom is "the truth in which the supreme good is discerned and possessed."[7]

With this description in mind, Augustine later remarks: "Happy indeed is he who is enraptured by the hightest good. For here is the truth that reveals [ostendit] all things that are really good, so that each man according to his lights selects one or more of them for his enjoyment."[8] If one understands the good in terms of perfection and if things basically appear in consciousness as finite and limited, then one could again argue that Augustinian wisdom is a basic a priori mediating context for the appearance of things in consciousness.[9] But apart from Augustine's proto-Kantian interpretation that will later collide with Kant's strictures on metaphysics, can one not recognize in Augustine's description of truth—as the light in which all other truths are seen—the *ratio entis*, that is, the object of intellection into which Aquinas says that we resolve all of our concepts?[10]

Also, in the first way to God in his *De Mysterio Trinitatis*, q. 1, a. 1, Bonaventure, a contemporary of Aquinas, says that we experience all things as limited in truth, perfection, and in ability to give peace or happiness. He regards this psychic dissatisfaction as an indication that we know all things within the context of eternal and infinite good, perfection, and happiness. Earlier in chapter III of his *Itinerarium Mentis in Deum* Bonaventure reiterates many of the above reductions of the finite to the infinite but regards their conclusions as a being—God. Also, as Augustine interpreted the light of truth as a constitutive a priori, Bonaventure does the same for our knowledge of God. Bonaventure says, "It remains, therefore, that the being which we are considering is the Divine Being. Strange, then, is the blindness of the intellect which does not consider that which it sees before all others and without which it can recognize nothing. . . . It comes first to the mind, and through it, all other things."[11]

Again, absent the identification with the divine being and absent the a priori interpretation, could not the roles that Bonaventure assigns the eternal and infinite good, perfection, and happiness be assumed, at least provisionally, by what Aquinas calls the *abstractum* of being? As explained, one must understand the notion of being as the sum total of all conceivable perfection. In that guise, the notion of being can certainly haunt our consciousness and spur the psychic restlessness noted by Bonaventure.

In my opinion, all of these thinkers are talking about the same thing—the presence in our consciousness of an intellectual sky against which everything else is profiled. It is true that these thinkers will go on to give different interpretations of this object, but what matters is to recognize that they are all gazing upon the same object and that they give witness to it.

Finally, lest one think that this intellectual sky is a phenomenon only for Christian thinkers, I would note that, like Augustine later, the ancient Greek philosopher Plato, in his dialogue, the *Republic* V (476 AD), spoke of all the intelligible forms participating in the light of the good. Also, Aristotle was Aquinas' source for the point that the *ratio entis*, unlike a genus, is not added to from the outside.[12] Also, Aristotle had a supreme philosophical science focused on being. But, anticipating the sameness-in-difference definition of the description of the Thomists, Aristotle insisted, at the beginning of *Metaphysics* IV, that being is said in many ways yet not "ambiguously" and not to the detriment of a "common notion or nature" of being.[13] In truth, the Christian medievals were trying to develop theses already found in pagan philosophy.

3. Being, the Good, and the Intellector of Being

But I want to return to Aquinas at 94, 2. As far as I know, only Aquinas explains how to integrate this unsurpassed object of natural human intellection with the human dignity that is crucial for a correct philosophical ethics and a correct notion of tolerance. Aquinas further describes being as the good. By *the good*, Aquinas also means the notion of being, the *ratio entis*, which he also mentions as the basis of the first principle of speculative reason—the principle of contradiction. It makes sense to call being the good because of the previously mentioned intelligible richness. Aquinas says that if we can call some individual thing good because it has certain perfections, then we can call being *the* good because it has all conceivable perfections.[14]

It could be objected that this characterization of being as the good is arbitrary. If the perfections of all things must be reduced into being like the analogates of any analogon, then the imperfections and defects of things should also be reduced into being. Are not the defects part of the very things that are analogates of being? It seems so. Hence the defects should also be read back into being and so compromise Aquinas' characterization of being as the good.

But this objection fails to see that evil arises from being only indirectly. Directly, only integral analogates arise from being. Evil occurs later when these integral analogates accidentally clash. For example, a tiger is an analogate of being and a human is an analogate of being. In their differences, both arise completely from the analogon. Trouble occurs when the human crosses the path of the tiger and has an arm ripped off. But all this evil is directly reduced only to the level of the analogates, not to the level of the analogon.

As I will explain in the next section, this same model can also explain moral evil among the analogates of being. For example, our sensitive nature with its appetites and our intellectual nature can be understood as analogates that integrally proceed from being. Sometimes, however, there can be a rush of sense appetite that clashes with what I intellectually know is bad for me. Because of the collision of sense appetite, what I know to be bad can at least *appear* as good. This resulting apparent good suffices for me to possibly choose it and so bring about a moral evil.

From his linking of being with the good, Aquinas deduces two things. The first is a necessary and automatic volition consequent upon the intellect's presentation of the *ratio boni* to the will. There is no moral necessity here because there is no freedom. The will acts automatically. According to Aquinas, the will automatically desires its proper object. At I, 82, 1c, Aquinas insists that natural necessity (*necessitas naturalis*) is not repugnant to the will. For just as the intellect of necessity adheres to first principles, so too the will necessarily adheres to the last end, which is happiness (*ultimo fini, qui est beatitudo*). But happiness here is the *ratio boni*, for elsewhere the last end is the object of the will (*rationem finis, est obiectum voluntatis*), and the object of the will is the *ratio boni* (*ratio boni, quod est obiectum potentiae*, I-II, 8, 2c).

Aquinas reiterates the point by saying that the will "tends naturally" (*naturaliter tendit*, I-II, 10, 1) to the *bonum in communi*, which is its object and last end, just as the intellect knows naturally the first principles of demonstration. Finally, that the *ratio entis* understood as the *ratio boni* engenders willing is also expressed in this Thomistic argument for will in God:

> From the fact that God is endowed with intellect it follows that He is endowed with will. For, since the understood good is the proper object of the will, the understood good is, as such, willed. Now that which is understood is by reference to one who understands. Hence, he who grasps the good by his intellect is, as such, endowed with will. But God grasps the good by His intellect. For, since the activity of His intellect is perfect, as appears from what has been said, He understands being together with the qualification of the good [*ens simul cum ratione boni.*]. He is, therefore endowed with will.[15]

No empty or merely formal sense of the *ratio boni* could play these roles of igniting volition. Rather, it is the *ratio entis* that is playing the role of the *ratio boni*.

The second implication of linking being with the good is the indeterminate disposing of the will before any individual thing that is only *a* good, not *the* good itself.

> So good is the object of the will. Therefore, if the will be offered an object which is good universally and from every point of view, the will tends to it of necessity, if it wills anything at all; since it cannot will the opposite. If, on the other hand, the will is offered an object that is not good from every point of view, it will not tend to it of necessity. And since the lack of any good whatever is a non-good, consequently, that good alone which is perfect and lacking in nothing is such a good that the will cannot not-will it: and this is happiness. But any other particular goods, in so far as they are lacking in some good, can be regarded as non-goods; and, from this point of view, they can be set aside or approved by the will, which can tend to one and the same thing from various points of view.[16]

Now the will is free, but moral constraint, or oughtness, still seems absent. Rather, what is present is an awareness of being equally and indifferently disposed to all finite goods. This freedom is known and understood as real and nonillusory because it has been built up from the *ratio entis*, whose objectivity is assured by its abstraction from the real beings given in sensation. Aquinas' direct realist epistemology regarding sensation has a crucial and basic role to play here.[17]

The issue remains. How are we to properly configure being as the good so that precisely moral obligation—not necessary volition or raw freedom—follows? In that way, one would understand "Good ought to be done" as self-evident, or *per se notum*. My resolution of the issue is the realization that Aquinas is not speaking of being as the good, pure and simple, but of being as the good when present in the human through the human's intellection of being.[18] Among all the instances of being as the good, the human, through intellection, has the good in an especially intense manner. Before such an instance, we are undoubtedly free, but we are also morally constrained. In the human, the *ratio boni* burns more brightly than it does in other instances such as animals, plants, and minerals. Does not that fact issue to our freedom a command of respect and solicitude? In sum, the subject of the first practical principle should not be understood simply as the good but as the good intellected by the human.

A text from the *Summa Contra Gentiles* provides textual confirmation for my process-of-elimination interpretation regarding the nature of the subject in the first practical principle. At book III, chapter 112, Aquinas is discussing God's providence over rational creatures. Aquinas wants to make the point that in His governance, God provides for rational creatures for their own sake and not for the sake of something else. Providence for the sake of something else characterizes God's governance of plants and animals. Plants are for the sake of animals, and animals are for the sake of humans. In chapter 112, Aquinas offers many arguments for God's governing humans for their own sake.

One argument is striking for the connection made between a metaphysical understanding of the human and obligation:

> Furthermore, it is evident that all parts are ordered to the perfection of the whole, since a whole does not exist for the sake of its parts, but, rather, the parts are for the whole. Now, intellectual natures have a closer relationship to a whole than do other natures; indeed, each intellectual substance is, in a way, all things. For it may comprehend the entirety of being [*totius entis comprehensiva*] through its intellect; on the other hand, every other substance has only a particular share in being. Therefore, other substances may fittingly be providentially cared for by God for the sake of intellectual substances.[19]

Aquinas starts by noting that parts are for the sake of their wholes. But an intellectual substance is more like a whole than a part thereof because the intellectual substance knows the whole of being (*totius entis*). Hence, in his governance, God provides for the sake of intellectors themselves. Notice Aquinas' deduction of obligation from a very metaphysical basis. God must or should treat the intellector in a particular way. In this case, the reason for the obligation is the understanding of the intellectual substance as an intellector of being. But the intellector-of-being conception is closely related to the intellector-of-the-good conception because being is not just any whole, or entirety, but the entirety of perfection. Hence, it is not surprising that even a creaturely intellector of being would command respect. So *Summa Contra Gentiles* III, 112, in my opinion, catches Aquinas doing what I claimed necessary to understand the subject of the first practical principle so that the subject contains the predicate of oughtness.

Aquinas' philosophical explanation of the initial phenomenon of obligation stands in opposition to David Hume's famous fact/value distinction. The eighteenth-century British philosophical skeptic David Hume claimed, "Take an action allowed to be vicious: willful murder, for instance. Examine it in all lights, and see if you can find that matter of fact, or real existence, which you call vice. In which ever way you take it, you find only certain passions, motives, volitions and thoughts. There is no other matter of fact in the case."[20] In short, calling an act "evil" denotes nothing in the act, nothing objective. "Evil" denotes something in us, something subjective—our emotion of revulsion. Of course, for Aquinas, another matter of fact exists in the act of murder. The victim is an intellector of being as the good. In light of that fact, the moral viciousness of killing is patent in the act itself. In striking at the person, the murderer is striking at the good.

So the first rule of a moral life is to be respectful and solicitous of the human person. The moral life is a life of love. The human person is the lighthouse from which shines the good and to which we should direct our moral vessel. For example, the immorality of murder, theft, and lying is patent. In striking at the person, each of these actions strikes unseemly at the good. Also, our awareness of ourselves as intellectors of being creates the injunctions to do what respects our existence and to avoid what disrespects it—for example, by abuse and suicide.

Moreover, the sexual embrace is unique among human physical activities. The sexual embrace is essentially unitive and procreative. By *essentially*, I mean the way an open and extended hand is in itself an act of friendship even if the hand is offered by a conniving politician. Hence, in one's sexual partner and also in the procreative teleology of the sexual embrace, one is handling the good. Therefore, sexual activity ought to be exercised in the context of a committed monogamous relationship—that is, within marriage. The fornicator and the adulterer unseemly discard that *ratio boni* given in the sexual embrace.

The evil of contraception is likewise evident. By striking at the procreative powers, contraception strikes both at the *ratio boni* that the sexual embrace intends to be given in one's partner and at the *ratio boni* in the offspring who is at least essentially, if not actually, present. Great lovers take this norm of respect and solicitude of the human person with deep seriousness. Their most important thing is other people, or life in society. Nothing should be substituted for people and their well-being—not hobbies, studies, pleasure, money, fame, or anything else. Pursuit of these things must always defer to the needs of persons.

Aquinas' conception of the human as an intellector of being also makes understandable the self-sacrifice involved in friendship. Following Aristotle, Aquinas roots friendship in self-love.[21] Self-love is not an egotistic predicament. What I find loveable in myself—the notion of being—is found in others. Being offers itself to all intellectors. Hence, my fellow is another self. In this context, my loss should not be looked at simply as another's gain. To see the other as a friend is to see my loss for his sake as *our* gain. Love for self extended to others makes it possible to genuinely rejoice in their good fortune, even when that good fortune demands a sacrifice from us. Jealousy should have no place among people if they relate to each other as friends. And people should relate to others as friends if they view themselves as intellectors of being. The deep truth here is indicated by its contrary—rejection and its lacerating effect of isolation. Since being is so intensely present in our fellows, then their rejection of us can appear as being's rejection of us. And since being includes all, rejection can be experienced as total isolation. That is why, though we may disagree, we should always remain friends.

4. Evil and the Intellector of Being

In sum, the above shows that, for Aquinas, reality itself prompts us to love. His epistemology of intellectual abstraction from the real things given to us in sensation establishes confidence in the notion of being. Being is not a pipe dream but a deep plunge into reality. Being's engendered command for respectful and solicitous treatment of our fellows as intellectors of being rings in our awareness with the sound of truth. In Thomistic psychology, love is not to suffer a delusion. Reality itself provides the motivation. But as so relentlessly developed from the real, Aquinas' ethics prompts another question. If we are structured as Aquinas says, why is human experience marked by so much hate and disrespect?

Some explanation of how Aquinas can be so right and yet things can be so wrong is desirable. How does perversity enter the life of an intellector of being? This discussion is important not only as a complement to Aquinas' philosophical psychology; the discussion will also be invaluable for grounding the possibility of dialogue with those who disagree with Aquinas' natural law ethics. Such a dialogue is essential equipment for any would-be Thomist, as he ponders going forth into his cultural milieu. Hence, I turn to another natural law text, *Summa Theologiae* I–II, 94, 6. Its topic is whether the natural law can be obliterated from the heart of man.

Aquinas first distinguishes natural law into the most common precepts known to all and secondary and more particular precepts that are conclusions following closely from the first principles. Aquinas' characterization of the most common precepts lets one coordinate them with the self-evident principles of natural law mentioned back at 94, 2. Chief among them is "Good ought to be done," which I glossed as "Be respectful and solicitous of intellectors of being." The other precepts of 94, 2—for example, "Respect oneself," "Respect one's sexual partner," "Respect one's fellow members of society," and "Respect one's intellection"— express heightened encounters with a person, and so are reducible to my interpretation of "Good ought to be done."

Aquinas says that these most common precepts, taken universally, cannot in any way be blotted out from men's hearts. However, their application to a particular action can be blotted out because of concupiscence or some other passion. What this brief remark means, Aquinas explains at length in a classic text on the genesis of the sinful act: *De Malo* I, 3c with parallel passages at *De Veritate*, XXIV, 8; *Summa Contra Gentiles* III, 10; and *Summa Theologiae* I, 63, 1. Aquinas' explanations are fascinating examples of a continued phenomenology of human consciousness. There are details of our psychology yet to be noticed, and these further details show how hate can blossom in a mind stamped by the intellection of being. I now turn to Aquinas on the causes of sin.

The key idea of understanding how the will introduces evil into its choices is the will's "nonconsideration of the rule" (*non consideratio regulae*). What is this? First, the nonconsideration cannot be a total and complete cognitive absence of the rule. If the nonconsideration were a complete absence, then the will would do evil without any awareness that it was doing evil. This unawareness would mean that the will's act was not a fault or a sin. Why? To sin means to do evil voluntarily. But voluntary action means action both with knowledge and with will. Hence, to sin, the will must have some awareness of the object as evil, and this awareness requires some recognition of the rule.

Second, neither can the rule be completely present in our awareness. A complete cognitive presence of the rule would extinguish from the object of an evil choice any and all appearance of good with the result that the object is impossible to choose. For Aquinas, a minimal condition for our willing anything, even something evil, is that the thing at least *appears* as good. Elsewhere, Aquinas gives his reason. His reason refers back to his psychology of willing that I described earlier: "The will naturally tends to good as its object. That it sometimes tends to evil happens only because the evil is presented to it under the aspect of good."[22] In contrast to us in this life, the blessed in heaven in the Beatific Vision have the rule of the good completely present in their consciousness. Consequently, the blessed apprehend all other things as they should be apprehended. Evil appears as the evil that it is and good appears as the good that it is. Because evil always appears as it is, evil never exercises any attraction over the wills of the blessed. In short, for the blessed, evil is never a possible object of choice.

So, the nonconsideration of the rule must mean an incomplete cognitive presence of the rule in virtue of which evil can *appear* as good though still be *known* as evil. In sum, Aquinas says, "Consequently there cannot be any sin in the motion of the will so that it tends to evil unless there previously exists some deficiency in the apprehensive power, as a result of which something evil is presented as good."[23] Now, what is the rule? Using what I have said in the third section above, the answer will be that the rule is the practical precept to be respectful and solicitous of the human understood as an intellector of being. The imperfect cognitive presence of this rule allows evil at least to appear as good and so make possible the evil choice.

Earlier at *De Veritate* XXIV, 8, Aquinas provides two reasons for this imperfect cognitive presence of the rule. The first reason is our passions, or sense appetites. The passions can arise so that what we saw as evil becomes only known as evil while taking on the appearance of good. For example, in my calm deliberation in the doctor's office and in the light of the norm of respect and solicitude for the human, my continual self-abuse by stuffing myself with refined carbohydrates appears as the evil that it is. Yet when I pass a bakery and smell the wonderful products inside, there is a rush of sense appetite for what I intellectually know is bad for me. In the context of that passion, what I know from memory to be bad (bad for me, at least), appears as good, and this is sufficient for me to possibly choose it and so bring about a moral evil. I can do what I know to be wrong. The passion never obliterates my previous knowledge of the baked goods as evil even while they are appearing as good. Their appearance as good is the erroneous judgment that Aquinas says is necessary for the evil act.[24]

For humans, the passions are a major source of evil acts. Because passions follow sense apprehension, we can be bombarded by things that incite all kinds of passions that invest something bad—because it is not in line with the first practical precept—with the appearance of good. This is even more evident for us who live in a media culture.

But passion cannot be the complete explanation for the nonconsideration of the rule. Besides committing crimes of passion, we also commit cold-blooded murder. Moreover, for the theologian Thomas Aquinas, not only humans are sinners but also the angels are sinners. But angels are incorporeal beings and so lack the sense appetites that are the passions. In other words, what is the form of the nonconsideration of the rule that applies to intellectual creatures as intellectual? Aquinas presents another way sin can take place. Since this way is more common, shared by us and by the angels, this way is the more profound explanation of how evil acts of will can take place. Aquinas says that, in this second case, "sin does not presuppose ignorance but merely absence of the consideration of the things which ought to be considered."[25] And elsewhere he says that, for this mere absence of consideration, the freedom of the creature suffices: *ad hoc sufficit ipsa libertas voluntatis.*

By mentioning the creature's freedom, Aquinas is referencing the will's state of indifference to all finite things thanks to their profiling against being as the good. Earlier, I mentioned this point, and I noted the state's absence of obligation, or moral necessity. In this state, I am before all things with complete indifference. I am in this state before I become aware of obligation, and I slip back into it after becoming aware of obligation. To use some terminology from computer programming, this state is the "default position" for the human creature. The appearance of obligation expressed in the first practical precept requires further concentration.

This is understandable in terms of Aquinas' epistemology. To initially grasp obligation, we have to grasp ourselves as intellectors of being as the good. But our cognitive attention is first directed to things. The knower is known subsequently by a reflection from things to the knower.[26] This reflection is a mental effort over and beyond our original knowledge of things and the presence of being in them. So it is not strange for Aquinas to say that the "soul does not hold nor is it able to actually hold always the rule." We can let the thought—of the rational creature as an epiphany of being—slip out of focus. When that happens, we revert to the prior state of freedom. In that state, things are no longer seen against the rule but are seen only against the *ratio entis.* This will mean that things not good in relation to the rule will still appear good in relation to being. As such, they are possible objects of choice, and if chosen, evil will be done.

So the "defect" here is an absence of consideration of the rule. This "defect" is not so much a defect that it becomes an evil. A true evil is a lack of something that should be there, such as lack of sight in a man (but not lack of sight in a rock). But the absence of consideration of the rule should be there so that the creature is free and freedom is a good. Yet the absence is not so natural that it escapes the will, for the will acts in this state with the knowledge that it could, and should, act with a consideration of the rule.

In conclusion, by the above phenomenology, we achieve a more balanced view of human nature. The first practical precept of respect and solicitude of the human is not so emblazoned in human consciousness that it cannot slip from focus. Passions can distract us and our natural state of freedom can cause a lack of consideration. Both allow what we know to be evil to take on the appearance of good. That cognitive state sets the stage for a possible act of evil by the will. So it is no sure thing that humans will do the good.

NOTES:

[1] Aquinas, *De Veritate* I, 12c. and XV, 1c.

[2] Most Thomists regard the principle as merely formal. For a survey, see Knasas, *Being and Some Twentieth-Century Thomists* (New York: Fordham University Press, 2003), 262, n. 22.

[3] James Anderson's terminology from his *The Bond of Being: An Essay on Analogy and Existence* (New York: Greenwood, 1969), 256.

[4] Gerald B. Phelan, "St. Thomas and Analogy," ed. by Arthur G. Kirn, in *G. B. Phelan: Selected Papers* (Toronto: Pontifical Institute of Mediaeval Studies, 1967), 114. Joseph Owens, "Analogy as a Thomistic Approach to Being," *Mediaeval Studies* 24 (1962): 308–309; also Joseph Owens, *An Elementary Christian Metaphysics* (Houston: Center for Thomistic Studies, 1985), 88, n. 14. Note that these Thomists describe the notion of being as a sameness-in-difference. This description does not say that sameness *is* the difference or that the difference *is* the sameness. To utter either of these would be to utter obvious contradictions. Rather, the Thomists claim that sameness was *in* the difference and that the difference was *in* the sameness. Neither of these claims is obviously a contradiction.

[5] On the terminology of analogon and analogate, see George P. Klubertanz, *St. Thomas on Analogy* (Chicago, IL: Loyola University Press, 1960), 6–7.

[6] Augustine, *De Libero Arbitrio*, bk. II, ch. 12; trans. John Wippel and Alan Wolter, *Medieval Philosophy from St. Augustine to Nicholas of Cusa* (New York: Free Press, 1969), 78.

[7] Ibid., 72

[8] Ibid., 78

[9] Despite these texts, Frederick Copleston, *A History of Philosophy* (Garden City, NY: Image Books, 1962) vol. 2, part 1, argues that, although the light of truth is an effect of God in the human mind, God in bestowing this light performs no "ideogenetic" function in regard to "the idea of beauty or any other normative idea (i.e., in reference to which we make

comparative judgments of degree, such as that this object is more beautiful than that, this action juster than that, etc.) ready-made into the mind" (p. 79). Rather the function of illumination is "regulative" of content received from the senses. Hence, "though Augustine does not clearly indicate *how we obtain* the notions of seven and three and ten, the function of illumination is not to infuse the notions of these numbers but so to illuminate the judgment that seven and three make ten that we discern the necessity and eternity of the judgment" (p. 80). But what Copleston points out is not the entire story. In the *De Libero Arbitrio* (Wippel and Wolter, *Medieval Philosophy*, 71) Augustine does argue that since arithmetical propositions are forever true, then they cannot be derived from sense, even if I perceived numbers by sense. But in the same place, Augustine adds that "one" is the principle of all number and "the perception of 'one' occurs through no bodily sense." So in this case at least, divine illumination accounts both for the quality and the content of the truth.

[10] Despite some apparent remarks to the contrary, for Aquinas, intellectual light is not like colored light. Unlike colored light, the agent intellect for Aquinas projects no content. On the contrary, at *Summa Theologiae* I, 79, 3c, Aquinas describes the working of the agent intellect, not in terms of an addition, but in terms of a subtraction. Just as natural light separates things from darkness, so too the agent intellect separates the forms of natural things from the "darkness" of matter. For commentary on the apparently contrary remarks at *De Veritate*, 10, 6c and ad 6m and at *Commentary on the Metaphysics of Aristotle* IV, lectio 6, see Knasas, *Being and Some Twentieth-Century Thomists*, 58–59.

[11] Bonaventure, *Itinerarium Mentis in Deum*, trans. and commentary by Philotheus Boehner (Saint Bonaventure, NY: The Franciscan Institute, Saint Bonaventure University, 1956), ch. 5, 83.

[12] "But it is not possible that either unity or being should be a single genus of things; for the differentiae of any genus must each of them both have being and be one." Aristotle, *Metaphysics* III, 3, 998b 22; as translated by W. D. Ross in Richard McKeon's edition, *The Basic Works of Aristotle* (New York: Random House, 1970), 723.

[13] "There are many senses in which a thing may be said to 'be', but all that 'is' is related to one central point, one definite kind of thing, and is not said to 'be' by a mere ambiguity. Everything which is healthy is related to health, one thing in the sense that it preserves health, another in the sense that it produces it, another in the sense that it is a symptom of health, another because it is capable of it. . . . As, then, there is one science which deals with all healthy things, the same applies in the other cases also. For not only in the case of things which have one common notion does the investigation belong to one science, but also in the case of things which are related to one common nature; for even these in a sense have one common notion. It is clear then that it is the work of one science also to study the things that are, *qua* being." Aristotle, *Metaphysics* IV, 2, 1003a 12–1003b 16; McKeon, *Basic Works of Aristotle*, 732. For this manner of conceptualizing a commonality, see the discussion of the Aristotelian equivocals in Joseph Owens, *The Doctrine of Being in the Aristotelian Metaphysics* (Toronto: Pontifical Institute of Mediaeval Studies, 1963), 112–115, 126–135.

[14] "But everything is perfect so far as it is actual. Therefore it is clear that a thing is perfect in so far as it is a being." *Summa Theologiae* I, 5, 1c.

[15] Aquinas, *Summa Contra Gentiles* I, 72, *Ex hoc*; trans. by Anton C. Pegis, *Summa Contra Gentiles*, (Notre Dame, IN: University of Notre Dame Press, 1975), vol. 1, pp. 239–240.

[16] Aquinas, *Summa Theologiae* I–II, 10, 2c; ed. by Anton C. Pegis, *The Basic Writings of St. Thomas Aquinas* (New York: Random House, 1945), vol. 2, p. 262.

[17] For a description and defense of Aquinas' sense realism, see Knasas, *Being and Some Twentieth-Century Thomists*, chs. 3, 4, and 9.

[18] See Knasas, *Being and Some Twentieth-Century Thomists*, 261–272.

[19] Aquinas, *Summa Contra Gentiles* III, 112, *Praeterea*; trans. Bourke, *Summa Contra Gentiles*, vol. 3.1, pp. 116–117.

[20] David Hume, *A Treatise of Human Nature*, bk. III, 1; Green and Grose ed., *David Hume: The Philosophical Works* (Darmstadt: Scientia Verlag Aalen, 1964), vol. 2, p. 245.

[21] See James McEvoy, "The Other as Oneself: Friendship and Love in the Thought of St. Thomas Aquinas," in *Thomas Aquinas: Approaches to Truth*, edited by James McEvoy and Michael Dunne (Dublin: Four Courts Press, 2002).

[22] Thomas Aquinas, *De Veritate* XXIV, 8c; trans. by Robert W. Schmidt, *The Disputed Questions on Truth* (Chicago, IL: Henry Regnery, 1954), vol. 3, p. 169.

[23] Ibid.

[24] "The fact that something appears good in the particular to the reason, which yet is not good, is due to a passion; and yet this particular judgment [*iudicium*] is contrary to the universal knowledge of reason." Aquinas, *Summa Theologiae* I-II, 77, 2, ad 2m; Pegis ed., *Basic Writings of St. Thomas Aquinas*, vol. 2, p. 634.

[25] Aquinas, *Summa Theologiae* I, 63, 1, ad 4m; trans. by Pegis, *Basic Writings*, vol. 1, p. 587.

[26] See Aquinas, *Commentary on the Metaphysics of Aristotle* XII, lect. 11, no. 2608, on Aristotle's remark: "But science, perception, opinion and thought always seem to be about something else and only indirectly about themselves." Of course, as subsistent forms, angels know in the opposite manner. They first know themselves and their ideas and then other things. Hence, the "default" position of their awareness is different. It is a knowledge of creation that does not include the creator's decisions about supernatural elevation. The divine announcement of those decisions is over and above the angel's natural knowledge. Hence, things can appear as good to the angel while still being known as possibly out of sync with the creator's de facto providence. The angel would sin by choosing without regard and deference for the creator's designs. See *Summa Theologiae* I, 63, 1. For commentary, see "Appendix 2" in Blackfriars' translation of the *Summa Theologiae* (New York: Mc-Graw-Hill Book Company, 1968), 311–320, and Jacques Maritain, *The Sin of the Angel* (Westminster, MD: Newman Press, 1959).

III

THE REALISM OF NATURAL LAW

As interesting and as probing as the above psychology is, it still smacks of unreality. The reason for this impression is that the sinner about whom Aquinas is talking is someone who already knows Aquinas' ethics. Some humans may be this kind of sinner. But what about most humans? Most seem to have no cognizance of the connection between "oughtness" and the human as intellector of being. So the drama of human life still escapes Aquinas' analyses. Better to turn to an existentialist like Heidegger or Marcel or Kierkegaard to supplement what appears as a kind of naivety in Aquinas.

In fact, Aquinas forces the issue. Again, at *Summa Theologiae* I-II, 94, 6c, Aquinas makes this claim: "As to common principles, the natural law, in its universal meaning, cannot in any way be blotted out from men's hearts."[1] Also, in article 2, he compares the first principle of practical reason to the first principle of speculative reason, the noncontradiction principle: "*The same thing cannot be affirmed and denied at the same time*, which is based on the notion of *being [rationem entis]* and *not-being*."[2] But as so based, the noncontradiction principle is self-evident not just in itself (*quoad se*), but for us too (*quoad nos*).[3] Moreover, in article 3 of question 94, Aquinas describes the common principles both of speculative and practical reason as "equally known to all [*apud omnes, et aequaliter nota*]."

So, even apart from my metaphysical gloss of 94, 2, in our day, can we agree that the primary precepts of Aquinas' natural law are known to all? How do proponents of euthanasia respect their own existence? How do proponents of recreational sex acknowledge its procreative and unitive nature? How do institutions of higher learning continue to acknowledge the intrinsic value of knowing, never mind the truth about God? Finding answers to these questions will take us deeper into Aquinas' philosophical psychology. The intellectual character of Aquinas' position should not be held against it, for Aquinas does not equate something being self-evident *quoad nos* with one's explicit acknowledgment of the item. Like the human heart that functions automatically but with conscious effects, so too, the intellect can automatically abstract the notion of being and grasp it as the good. Such an automatic abstraction can go a long way toward explaining why people try to avoid contradiction, yearn for something that life cannot give, and experience freedom (and also obligation). Evidently we know more than we are aware of knowing.

1. Primary Precepts and Levels of Self-Evidency

Despite the *quoad nos* self-evident character of the primary practical precepts, Aquinas holds a dim view of the workings of the intellect. For example, in the *Summa Contra Gentiles* III, 26, he explains that it is not strange that humans act for sensual pleasures rather than intellectual ones because most humans lack intellectual experience. For this lack, Aquinas appeals to his abstractionist epistemology. He says that external things are better known because human cognition begins from sensible things.[4] Later in the same work (at IV, 52), he speaks of the "frailty of reason [*debilitas rationis*]" and of the predominance of the phantasms. But instead of contradicting Aquinas' position that the primary precepts are known to all, these remarks produce a better understanding of Aquinas' position. For one would be wrong to interpret these remarks to mean that the workings of the intellect are totally absent or that these workings have no experienced effects.

Even on the level of sensation, we know more than we are aware of knowing. Sense has a focus that is narrower that its entire field. For example, my vision is giving me a dozen objects yet my awareness does not yet include that number. For Aquinas, a similar relation can exist between sensation and intellection. Even though our attention is focused on sensible things, our intellection has gone on to grasp commonalities of which we are still unaware. How else does one explain that we abide by the noncontradiction principle, are inevitably dissatisfied by finite goods, and know that we are free in respect to anything in our experience? These phenomena show that the notion of being haunts the human mind. A clever Thomist would seize upon each phenomenon to lead the person to realize something that the person in fact already knows—the notion of being and the understanding of being as the good. So much of Thomism is making the implicit explicit (to rob some language from Transcendental Thomism).

Furthermore, as mentioned in chapter II above,[5] our awareness of things and the intelligibilities that things contain is never so focused that all self-awareness is lost. Hence, we cannot but have some awareness of ourselves as intellectors of being. So, with avoidance of contradiction, with yearning, and with freedom, the phenomenon of obligation is another outcropping indicating the presence of the *abstractum* of being in the depths of human consciousness. Again, we know more than we are aware of knowing. While our attention is on sensible things, or phantasms, the intellect can be doing its own work with the mentioned results.

So, a Thomist is not upset that most people appear to be living with no awareness of themselves as intellectors of being. In the Thomist's contemplation of his fellows, the knowledge of themselves as intellectors of being is present and is explaining their inchoate sense of their own dignity. This inchoate sense of dignity appears in proponents of euthanasia who point out the indignity of a long, lingering, painful death. Even proponents of recreational sex acknowledge it when they insist that recreational sex is morally acceptable because "no one is getting hurt" and it involves only "consenting adults."

A Thomist will continue to regard euthanasia and recreational sex as morally abhorrent, but that dislike should not cause him to miss a concession to his understanding of the value of the human person. Furthermore, the Thomist's understanding of human epistemology allows the Thomist to understand the genesis of the moral confusion. His opponent knows that he ought to respect himself and others but does not know why. And the opponent does not know why because the opponent still lacks an awareness of his apprehension of being as the good. The awareness is lacking because, even though intellection has already discerned in external sensible things the notion of being, attention is focused on the sensible things. With only a superficial grasp of themselves, people can honestly believe that they are respecting their dignity when tragically they are not.

So even though the primary precepts are *per se notum quoad nos*—self-evident to all—it does not follow that all are equally aware of the meaning of the subjects. In the case of the primary precept, "The human ought to be treated with respect and solicitude," the subject is the human person. In light of Aquinas' abstractionist epistemology, is it not possible to have varying depths of understanding of this subject? Can it not be the case that we are intellectors of being long before we become aware of that fact? An affirmative reply would explain why most people experience obligation both to themselves and their fellows yet can be so confused about the particulars of this obligation.

That confusion would also explain why these people go on to miss knowledge of the secondary precepts of natural law. Hence, at *Summa Theologiae* I–II, 94, 4c, Aquinas mentions Caesar's observation of the approval of theft among the Germans. The Germans permitted armed robbery of others outside the tribe. The basic reason appears to be their paranoid opinion that outsiders were potential enemies. This opinion is indicative of a shallow understanding of what lies in the depths of the human person.

2. The Primary Precept to Know God

Aquinas' distinction between what we know about ourselves and what we realize about ourselves helps us understand another primary precept mentioned by Aquinas at 94, 2: "Divine truth ought to be sought." Along with other primary precepts, Aquinas says that this one has universal truth and is *per se notum quoad nos*. But is it clear that God exists and, even if it is clear, is it clear that we ought to concern ourselves with knowing God? How does a primary precept about God arise in Aquinas' natural law?

Earlier in his *Summa Contra Gentiles* III, 38, Aquinas describes an ordinary knowledge of God possessed by all mature human beings. Perhaps it will answer my questions. This ordinary knowledge of God is a posteriori and appears to recount a primitive version of the teleological argument. It runs as follows:

> What seems indeed to be true [is] that man can immediately reach some sort of knowledge of God by natural reason. For, when men see that things in nature run according to a definite order, and that ordering does not occur without an orderer, they perceive in most cases that there is some orderer of the things that we see. But who or what kind of being, or whether there is but one orderer of nature, is not yet grasped immediately in this general consideration . . . . But this knowledge admits of a mixture of many errors. Some people have believed that there is no other orderer of worldly things than the celestial bodies, and so they said that the celestial bodies are gods. Other people pushed it further, to the very elements and the things generated from them, thinking that motion and the natural functions which these elements have are not present in them as the effect of some other orderer, but that other things are ordered by them. Still other people, believing that human acts are not subject to any ordering, other than human, have said that men who order others are gods. And so, this knowledge of God is not enough for felicity.[6]

Aquinas concedes that the argument has many shortcomings. For example, Aquinas notes that one does not yet grasp who or what is this orderer of if the orderer is one or many. On the strength of this argument, some identify the orderer with the heavenly bodies, the elements, or other human beings. But does not Aquinas' concession contradict his thesis that men are knowing God? None of the characterizations of the orderer are remotely similar to the God of Aquinas' religious belief who is spiritual, unique, and nonhuman. Would it not have been clearer for Aquinas to say that men fail to attain a knowledge of God? In other words, when a physicist discovers a new particle, he does not exclaim "God." And if he did, we would think him strange. Hence, is not Aquinas odd to attribute man's knowledge of God to man's knowledge of the elements? In fact, on another occasion, Aquinas is uncompromising, if not uncharacteristically cruel, in his dismissal of David of Dinant's identification of God with matter.[7]

Returning to the *Summa Contra Gentiles*, it is important to realize that Aquinas does not say that men reach something "like" God. Aquinas' assertion is unqualified. Men reach God, even though they take what they reach and identify it with the mentioned nondivine instances. Consequently, in the next chapter, when Aquinas introduces philosophical demonstrations to remove the errors, the removal does not consist in moving on to a higher being than those mentioned. Rather, the corrections consist in purifying, through removal of the errors, what the general reasoning had reached.[8] So, before this text on an ordinary knowledge of God can be used to support a universal knowledge of the primary precept obliging us to know divine truth, some explanation of how the conclusion of the reasoning can be so wrong and still be right is required. Here a return to Aquinas' abstractionist epistemology can be helpful.

According to Aquinas, the errors in man's ordinary knowledge of God are set aside by demonstration. The backward reference is important. Early in Book One, Aquinas reserves these points of demonstration to the last part of philosophy to be learned, namely, to metaphysics.[9] This assignment should mean that the ordinary knowledge of God is in some way metaphysical. Only as metaphysical could it successfully reach God, albeit imperfectly, as Aquinas claims. But can one possibly regard ordinary individuals to be in possession of Aquinas' metaphysics?[10]

3. Metaphysics as Implicit Knowledge

The key note in Aquinas' metaphysics is his understanding of the existence of the thing. Unlike in our common usage, in Aquinas' meta-physics, "the existence of the thing" does not mean simply the fact of the thing. Aquinas regards existence as a distinct principle or act composed with the individual substance to render the substance a being (*ens*), an existent. In fact, at *Summa Contra Gentiles* II, 54, the thing's existence is a sufficiently distinct principle so that Aquinas can compare its composition with a substance with form's composition with matter within the substance. Aquinas employs the phrase *actus essendi*, the act of being, and the Latin infinitive, *esse*, as a noun, or substantive, to express his unique act-sense of the thing's existence. It is not so much that Aquinas disagrees with the fact-sense of the thing's existence, but rather that Aquinas insists that the fact-sense be deepened to include the act in virtue of which the thing is a fact. A thing is a fact in virtue of its *actus essendi*. A being or an existent qua a being or an existent is a *habens esse*, a possessor of the act of being.

The relation of this act to the substance with which it is composed also bears mention. In respect to the substance rendered a being by com-position with *esse*, *esse* is prior (*prius*), first (*primus*), most profound (*profundius*), and most intimate (*magis intimum*). *Esse* is the core around which the thing revolves. We are so accustomed to perceiving acts of a thing as items subsequent and posterior to the thing that the notion of an act basic and fundamental to its thing is strange. But if one is to correctly appreciate *esse*, usual ways of thinking must be suspended.

As an act, *esse* is an *ipso facto* dependent item. No act as an act, even the sui generis act that is *esse* is found by itself. Rather, an act is found as in and of a subject. However, there is no way to explain *esse* completely by the substance that is its subject. Substances that are complete explainers of an act are in some respect already in act. As a potency for its existential act, substance cannot position itself to completely explain its *esse*. The need for complete explanation in the case of *esse* drives the mind to conclude to a further being in which *esse* is not found as an act but as the very substance that is the further cause.

Aquinas calls this further cause *esse subsistens* (subsistent exis-tence), *esse tantum* (existence alone), and *esse purum* (pure existence). He also refers to it as *Deus* (God). Aquinas' stated reason is God's revelation to Moses in the Book of Exodus that God's name is *Ego sum qui sum*: I am who am.[11] As subsistent *esse*, the first cause of *esse* embodies the key com-ponent in Aquinas' understanding of the notion of being, the *ratio entis*. Since the *ratio entis* is also the *ratio boni*, then the first cause is the preem-inent epiphany of the good among all such epiphanies. If the human commands respect and solicitude because the human, as an intellector of being, is an epiphany of the good, then a fortiori the first cause does likewise. In the light of Aquinas' metaphysics, to orient our moral compass to the divine instance is an obvious *per se notum* truth. This analysis also illustrates a profound opening in human subjectivity for the life of grace and its culmination in beatitude.

But again, is it plausible to regard Aquinas' metaphysics as a natural and automatic achievement that exists below the level of conscious articulation so that most will have a knowledge of God, imperfect as it is? The answer depends upon our access to the data in which are Aquinas' key metaphysical notions. The setting up of things in various multiplicities is the standard procedure for the discernment of the thing's acts.[12] For example, because I find the water both hot and cold, I come to discern the various temperatures as acts of the water that in itself is temperature neutral. Moreover, I come to understand each of the instances as a composition of the water plus some temperature. Likewise, because I can find Tom both pale and ruddy, I come to discern the complexions as acts of Tom who in himself is complexion neutral. But for Aquinas, things are found not only in temperature and complexion multiplicities but also in existential multiplicities.

Aquinas is an immediate realist in his understanding of sensation. Sensation provides not an image, a representation, a picture of the real thing, but the real thing itself. Consequently, the hot water and the pale Tom do not just really exist in my sensation, they also cognitionally exist. The presentation of some thing in an existential multiplicity should drive the mind to understand the thing to be in itself existence neutral and to understand each instance as a composition of the said thing plus a real or cognitional existence in the sense of an act.

The answer to the above question reduces to an answer to this question. Is the mentioned existential multiplicity available to the ordinary person? Certainly. No ordinary person doubts a real world in his sensation. No ordinary person questions the distinction between remembering their beloved in a memory versus being in the beloved's presence. Even though modern philosophy has run away from the immediate presence of the real in sensation, ordinary people continue to live according to that marvelous truth. Furthermore, ordinary people have sufficient presence of mind that none lack an awareness of their own sensation. Hence, they not only know real things, they know that they know real things. In other words, ordinary people not only sense real things, they also are aware that they sense real things. In short, there is every reason to think that the intellect not only discerns the notion of being, as I have claimed above, but that it also apprehends the notion of being in the sense of *habens esse*. The data is sufficiently available for the intellect to be led to the metaphysical distinction between a thing and its *esse*, even if our awareness is elsewhere.

But upon a grasp of the composition, cannot the intellect go on to grasp the conclusion that the *esse* is caused? One conscious outcrop of this activity is Leibniz's question of why there is something rather than nothing. As Heidegger points out at the very start of his *An Introduction to Metaphysics*, the question steals upon us in moments of despair, rejoicing, and boredom. Looked at Thomistically, Heidegger's remark makes sense. Common to these moods is the shutting down of our plans and designs so that we are left simply in the presence of things. But that hovering of things in our awareness bespeaks, as explained, an instability in existents that prompts Leibniz's question. Aquinas' metaphysics is as near as the sense realism of ordinary experience.

In my opinion, another indication is Aquinas' listing of identities for the orderers in this ordinary knowledge of God. All of these orderers are intensely related to the notion of being. I have spoken about the relation of the person to the notion of being. But even the contemplation of the heavens would impress the notion of being upon us. Because of their gargantuan dimensions, only the notion of being would allow us to profile the heavens in our mind. But such an intense presence of the notion of being might lead one to confuse the heavens with the cause of being. As mentioned, the notion of being harbors causal implications. Causality goes with the notion of being. In an ordinary person, these implications may not be sufficiently distinguished from the instance whose objectification makes the notion of being so necessary.

But if the physically great requires the notion of being, so too does the physically small. Hence, at *Summa Contra Gentiles* III, 38, Aquinas also mentions the identification of the divine with the elements. To contemplate the physically small, everything else must be removed from our awareness. That move leaves the physically small alone with the notion of being. The heightened presence of being in the contemplation of minutiae could lead one to confuse the causal implications with the minutiae themselves.

In sum, God can be confused with both the great and the small because the presence of the notion of being, in which there are causal implications, is so necessary for the contemplation both of the great and of the small. It is no surprise that people basically divide into those who like the mountains and those who like the shore. One looks at the expanse of the sky, the other at vessels on the vast ocean. As the Thomist considers both observers, the Thomist believes that the genuine object of the contemplation is being and that their relaxation is some approximation of the happiness that would be achieved in knowing being itself.

4. Self-Evidency and Burdens of Articulation

That the primary precept to know the truth about God is evident to all is important for another reason. Even though Aquinas says that demonstration in philosophy removes the errors in this ordinary knowledge of God, philosophy does not end all disputes about God. Because of the intrinsic difficulty of the task, various philosophies are likely to contain massive error. In fact, as I mentioned at the end of chapter I, Aquinas employs this observation to justify revelation nonredundantly including naturally knowable truths about God. So, no Thomist would be so naive as to think that labors come to an end after dealing with "ordinary" humans. The Thomist knows that fellow philosophers will also pose problems. Aquinas' admission of truths self-evident to all is not embarrassed by disagreement about those truths.

Consider also that, as noted above, at 94, 2, Aquinas also describes the first speculative principle—"A thing cannot both be and not be at the same time"—as both self-evident and known to us. But as indicated from his commentary on Aristotle's *Metaphysics*, Aquinas is not so naive as to believe that disputers are nonexistent. Aquinas knows that some deny the principle on the bases that contraries are seen to come from the same thing and that all opinions seem true.[13] Aquinas' admission here and his asserted parallelism between the speculative and practical areas at 94, 2, should mean that the first practical principle is not so self-evident *quoad nos* that deniers are rendered nonexistent.

Aquinas deals with deniers of the noncontradiction principle by pointing out that if they affirm anything, then they deny that reality is contradictory. The only way to keep their denial is to say nothing, and so they reduce themselves to the level of plants.[14] Transcendental Thomists especially claim that Aquinas' opponents can justifiably be construed as Kantian philosophers who wish to limit necessary ways of thinking just to ways of thinking instead of ways of really existing. But the opponents, as well as Aquinas and Aristotle, are all realists. The premise assumed by all parties is that thought is determined by the real. That is why Aquinas insists both that thought would be destroyed if reality is contradictory and that reality is consistent if thought is consistent.

Following Aristotle, Aquinas also goes on to address the above two reasons for the opposing opinion. By distinguishing being in potency from being in act, the phenomenon of contraries emerging from the same thing need not imply a denial of the noncontradiction principle.[15] Also, by noting how the sense organ can be affected by various dispositions, one can understand how different people would have different opinions.[16] My point here and now is not to defend Aquinas' replies. My point simply is to observe that Aquinas' thesis of the to-us-self-evident character of the noncontradiction principle is congruent with opposition. Evidently, Aquinas' position on the *per se notum quoad nos* character of some propositions is more nuanced than was at first presumed. Aquinas never understood the position to be open to embarrassment by opponents to it. Moreover, Aquinas' opponents are articulate, and so, proponents must appropriately meet them with counter articulation. It will not suffice simply to assert self-evidency.

5. A Commensurating Discourse

So, the primary precepts of Aquinas' natural law are known to all and possess a universal truth. Yet understanding this correctly requires a precision. This precision concerns the unequal knowledge of the subject of the precepts. For example, all have a sense of obligatory respect and solicitude towards themselves and others. That sense of obligation is what cannot be eliminated from the human heart. But few grasp that that respect stems from the human's status as an intellector of being. The disparity reduces to the fact that not all appreciate their own intellection. That failure, in its turn, is traced to the abstractive nature of intellection. What the intellect abstracts can be hidden from awareness by the data which is more out front in our awareness. Hence, some people can be honestly ignorant and confused about even the primary precepts of natural law. Their explicit knowledge of themselves can be so superficial that it will allow confusions about what is congruent or incongruent with human dignity. We need ascribe to them neither an ill will nor bad habits, though, as we have seen, Aquinas is fully cognizant of these factors. Weakness of reason suffices.[17]

In conclusion, the Neo-Thomist understanding of the human as an intellector of being need plead no excuse about handling subjectivity. From their understanding of Aquinas, these Thomists can locate enough material to show that the notion of being controls, and has always controlled, human psychology. Though not the entire story, the intellection of being is the central theme about the human. It is there when we are moral, and it is there when we are immoral. It is there when we understand, and it is there when we do not understand.

Fundamentally and always, even if we do not realize it, we face each other as fellow intellectors of being; that is the stage upon which human existence is played. In the light of this philosophical psychology, as well as the good news of the Christian faith which is a marvelous completion of this psychology, our would-be Thomist goes out to meet others. The Thomist will find thick walls of cultures or philosophies, but the walls will not be impenetrable. Aquinas' psychology provides a commensurating discourse. Being cannot be eliminated from the heart of the human.

NOTES:

[1] Anton C. Pegis, ed., *The Basic Writings of St. Thomas Aquinas* (New York: Random House, 1945), II, 781.

[2] Ibid., II, 774.

[3] "If, therefore, the essence of the predicate and subject be known to all, the proposition will be self-evident to all; as is clear with regard to the first principles of demonstration, the terms of which are certain common notions that no one is ignorant of, such as being [*ens*] and non-being . . ." Aquinas, *Summa Theologiae* I, 2, 1c; Pegis, ed., *Basic Writings*, I, 19.

[4] "Nor do more persons seek the pleasure that is associated with knowing rather than the knowledge. Rather, there are more people who seek sensual pleasures than intellectual knowledge and its accompanying pleasure, because things that are external stand out as better known, since human knowledge starts from sensible objects." *Summa Contra Gentiles* III, 26; trans. by Vernon J. Bourke, *Summa Contra Gentiles* (Notre Dame, IN: University of Notre Dame Press, 1975) III, part 1, 109–110.

[5] See chapter II, n. 26, above.

[6] Bourke, trans., *Summa Contra Gentiles*, III, part 1, 125–126.

[7] "The third error is that of David of Dinant, who most stupidly taught that God was primary matter." *Summa Theologiae* I, 3, 8c; Anton Pegis, ed., *Basic Writings of St. Thomas Aquinas*, I, 35.

[8] "On the other hand, there is another sort of knowledge of God, higher than the foregoing, and we may acquire it through demonstration. A closer approach to a proper knowledge of Him is effected through this kind, for many things are set apart from Him, through demonstration, whose removal enables Him to be understood in distinction from other beings. In fact, demonstration shows that God is immutable, eternal, incorporeal, altogether simple, one, and other such things which we have shown about God in Book One." Pegis, trans., *Summa Contra Gentiles*, III, part 1, 127. For a description of "removal" as the negating capacity of the mind's second operation and how it is wielded to chisel out a confused

knowledge of the divine quiddity, see Knasas, *Being and Some Twentieth-Century Thomists,* 236–244.

[9] "In order to know the things that the reason can investigate concerning God, a knowledge of many things must already be possessed. For almost all of philosophy is directed towards the knowledge of God, and that is why metaphysics, which deals with divine things, is the last part of philosophy to be learned." *Summa Contra Gentiles* I, 4; Anton Pegis, trans., *Summa Contra Gentiles* I, 67. In the previous chapter, naturally knowable truth about God includes the knowledge of his existence: "But there are some truths which the natural reason also is able to reach. Such that God exists, that He is one, and the like." Pegis, trans., *Summa Contra Gentiles,* I, 63.

[10] For the Thomistic texts behind the many points in the next section's description of Aquinas' metaphysics, see Knasas, *Being and Some Twentieth-Century Thomists,* chapters VI and VII.

[11] "This sublime truth Moses was taught by our Lord. When Moses asked our Lord: 'If the children of Israel say to me: what is His name? What shall I say to them?' The Lord replied: '*I am who am* . . . Thou shalt say to the children of Israel: *He who is* hath sent me to you' (Exod. 3:13, 14). By this our Lord showed that His own proper name is *He who is.* Now, names have been devised to signify the natures or essences of things. It remains, then, that the divine being is God's essence or nature." *Summa Contra Gentiles* I, 22, no. 10: Pegis, trans., *Summa Contra Gentiles,* I, 121.

[12] The following is a nontechnical paraphrase of Aquinas' approach to the *actus essendi* of a thing by the twofold operation of the intellect—conceptualization and judgment. For the twofold operation of the intellect presentation, see Knasas, *Being and Some Twentieth-Century Thomists,* 182–196.

[13] Aquinas, *Commentary on the Metaphysics of Aristotle* IV, *lectio* 10, no. 665 and *lectio* 11, nos. 669–670.

[14] Ibid., *lectio* 6, no. 608.

[15] Ibid., *lectio* 10, no. 667

[16] Ibid., *lectio* 11, no. 671.

[17] In his commentary on the third book of Aristotle's *Nicomachean Ethics* at *lectio* 3, n. 412, Aquinas agrees with Aristotle that universal ignorance does not excuse. As an example of universal ignorance, Aquinas cites being ignorant of the norm that fornication is always wrong. Does Aquinas mean that everyone should know that fornication is wrong so that if they do not, then they are blameworthy? I do not think so. In the preceding paragraph, no. 411, Aquinas makes the context clear. The ignorance that does not excuse belongs to a man "having the use of reason (*homini habenti usum rationis*)." But in my text above in section 3, I thought that I showed that, for Aquinas, few men fit that description. Rather, among men there is a *debilitas rationis* (*Summa Contra Gentiles* IV, 52) reflected in the fact that men abstractively draw their knowledge from phantasms. Hence, earlier (ibid., III, 26), because they are more obvious, phantasms are described as occluding an awareness of intelligibilities. That is why most men lack intellectual experience and satisfaction so that sense pleasure is predominantly pursued. So I do not think that an analogy exists between ordinary people and a third-grade student who is incorrectly doing simple addition. In the latter case, you can presume enough reason to hold the student responsible for his errors. But grasping the natural law precepts correctly is not as simple as that. Some intellectual sophistication is required and few have that. The rest of men bumble around and only vaguely understand their dignity with the result that they tragically judge some actually bad behaviors to be congruent with that dignity. In the context of all that, I interpret the fact that

Aquinas addresses their confusion intellectually indicates that the confusion is not a moral one, as he does the proponent of fornication at *Summa Contra Gentiles* III, 124, and the person in "universal ignorance" at *De Veritate* 24, 10. Aquinas also compares the "*malas persuasiones*"—by which some can be ignorant of the secondary precepts—to errors in speculative matters (*Summa Theologiae* I–II, 94, 6). But surely not all speculative errors are blameworthy. "*Malas*" does not have to mean "morally evil." For example, there can be natural evil, "*malum naturalis defectus*" at *Summa Theologiae* I, 19, 9c. Sometimes the intellect leads the will astray instead of the will leading the intellect.

IV

AQUINAS' NATURAL LAW AND TOLERANCE

I have explained in chapter II how, in his natural law ethics, Aquinas parlayed the already recognized medieval idea of the human as an intellector of being into the basis of obligation, or moral necessity. To appreciate oneself and others as intellectors of being is to realize that all ought to be treated with the respect and solicitude that is owed to the good itself. Moreover, I have also argued in chapter III that, despite a prima facie remoteness from the lives of ordinary people, Aquinas' philosophical psychology is ineluctable. The inescapability is rooted in the understanding that the intellect, like the human heart, can function so spontaneously that its workings escape notice, though they are not without conscious effects. Is not this Thomistic thesis an obvious basis for tolerance in the sense of mutual goodwill? And so here I want to explain first how the thesis engenders mutual goodwill for others in general. Second, in the second section of this chapter, I want to explain how it does the same for those with whom one disagrees. Third, in the third section below, I want to explain how Aquinas' thesis establishes mutual goodwill for others with whom one differs. Finally, I want to compare the possibilities for creativity and novelty that I find in Aquinas to another philosopher of being, Martin Heidegger.

1. Society and the Intellector of Being

So first, whether others see themselves as intellectors of being, that is how a Thomist regards them. And just as a Thomist welcomes being in his own intellection and cherishes himself in that light, so too a Thomist welcomes it in others. Because, through humans, being acquires a voice, a Thomist wants to live among others and not with rocks and trees. Society is a good. So too the Thomist wants to nurture the expression of being in his fellows. The Thomist not only wants to hear what others have to say but wants to help them to say it. These others can count on the Thomist's goodwill, as hopefully the Thomist can count on theirs. Aquinas' thinking fundamentally sets up human beings in a relation of mutual goodwill and fraternity. His thinking, then, obviously sets them up in a relation of tolerance.

What I have just said can be taken as a more profound reiteration of Aristotle's observation that, by nature, the human is a social animal. Because one alone is insufficient to provide for one's own needs and necessities, Aristotle presented life in society as a human good.[1] But meeting practicalities does not exhaust human life. In the *Metaphysics*, Aristotle keenly observed that practical success gave way to the free pursuit of knowledge.[2] As effective as Aristotle's external observation of knowledge for its own sake is,[3] a consideration of subjectivity more intimately confirms the same point. The intellection of being dares to explain from the inside the wonder that can burst forth from a well-ordered life.

Though perhaps not yet explicitly appreciated, the intellectual apprehension of the notion of being—the sameness through all differences and of which we want to know more by knowing more and more beings— is what creates the thirst for truth alone. Awareness of this deeper source of intellectual desire transforms our understanding of the basis of society. We are not condemned to know more of being by canvassing one dumb object after another, by adding one more rock or insect to our collections. In the intellection of our fellows, being has a heightened presence that gives it a voice. The desire to plumb the depths of being naturally leads to a desire to live among fellow intellectors of being. If the human is by nature an intellector of being, then logically the human is also a social animal.

But, if a Thomist is faithful to Aquinas' core ideas, the Thomist will understand that society is not simply for intellectual pursuit. Successful societies were around and have been around without having blossomed into philosophy as in Aristotle's example. The anthropological facts indicate that the longing to live uprightly is more primal than the longing for truth.[4] People in these nonphilosophical societies used their leisure to listen to stories celebrating the great deeds of ancestors. Through the witness of the lives of our fellows, society furnishes inspirations of living the moral life and so addresses a deep longing. Thomist psychology can assimilate this fact as well.

It is true that in chapter II's description of Aquinas' philosophical psychology, the notion of being is apprehended as an intelligible object before it is apprehended as a moral object. The line runs from the presentation of sense, to the intellection of being, to its apprehension as analogous, to its status as a transcendental, to its appreciation as the good, to ourselves as intellecting it as the good, and finally to the apprehension to be respectful and solicitous. In this line, purely intellectual considerations definitely precede moral considerations. But it is far from necessary that the transitions occur on the level of explicit consciousness.

While consciousness remains concentrated on sensible things, the intellect automatically and spontaneously has gone on to transit the above line. This understanding of what the intellect performs so naturally that it escapes consciousness would mean that what is closest to explicit understanding, or to consciousness, is not the start of the line but its end. In other words, moral considerations, not intellectual ones, would predominate in the awareness of ordinary people as cultural anthropology indicates. Since awareness would work from the end of the line to its start in the depths of human psychology, then awareness of intellection naturally would take time and emerge late and sporadically in human history.

2. Dialogue and the Intellector of Being

Second, worth noting is that Aquinas' basis for mutual respect is deeper and earlier than that of developed philosophies. Any person is already an intellector of being before that person is a philosopher who may happen to agree with a Thomist like me. So Aquinas' understanding of the respect owed to one's fellow intellector of being holds even when one's fellow formulates a philosophy at odds with Thomism. In other words, Aquinas' philosophical psychology does not allow for a chasm of incommensurability between philosophers. Somehow and somewhere, contact with another philosopher is possible no matter how discordant the philosophy, either speculative or practical, is from yours. Friendly and patient dialogue will eventually uncover the play of being in the philosopher's psyche so that further discussion will have a more commonly acknowledged focus.

So, by Aquinas' very ideas, a Thomist, in my opinion, is committed logically to behaving with respect. That one has known Thomists who have behaved otherwise—for example, solving philosophical disagreements by appeal to extra-philosophical means, such as insults or political intrigue—counts for nothing because anything good can be abused. Ideas should be judged for themselves, not by the behavior of those who espouse them. Otherwise the analysis becomes distressingly ad hominem.

That Aquinas' psychology finds a common denominator in all

human intellects does not mean that the Thomist naively presupposes good-will in others. As we saw in chapter III, Aquinas is quite aware of the play of emotions in human life such that bad choices can be made. But again, the most poignant effects of emotions are often in conjunction with being. The emotion of fear of loneliness and isolation, from which many moral compromises follow, results from the intense presence of being in one's fellows. That is why experiencing human rejection can seem like experiencing total rejection.

If one has only a vague sense of being and of one's own intellection of it, one can be tempted to think that one's worth is somehow tied up with the good estimate of others. A swelling of pride can also be occasioned by the notion of being insofar as a vague grasp of human psychology can take explicit understanding to be the only way of understanding. The boastful intellectual fails to realize that his glorious philosophy is only an explicit rendering of what is implicit in every human.

So Aquinas does not naively look at fellow humans simply as in-tellectors of being. He looks at them as intellectors of being that for all kinds of reasons can compromise themselves. But even in an intellector of being gone astray, we have an intellector of being. The challenge will be to find the opening to that intellectual achievement in the individual with whom one is living.[5] Even after successfully doing that, one knows that freedom remains. One knows that, even in calm deliberation, it is not pos-sible to always consider the rule, and so the husband can choose the illicit pleasure over the simply remembered norm of fidelity, and the intellectual can opt for espousing the group line rather than the truth as the intellectual sees it.

But one should be hopeful. Though Aquinas is no Platonist for whom knowledge is virtue, the presentation of the good in knowledge does have an effect. That is why Aquinas holds that the number of angels who remained firm is greater than the number of those who sinned.[6] I see in Aquinas no substantial obstacle to the project of continued intellectual en-gagement with one's fellows. As I explained in chapters II and III, despite our mistakes and immorality, we are all intellectors of being.

Aquinas witnesses this vocation. Aquinas understands philosophy to be a product of natural reason. But natural reason is a capacity to under-stand shared by all human beings. Hence, the only genuine way one can propagate Aquinas' natural law ethics is by addressing the natural reason of humans. Diamond must cut diamond. This task demands arduous, pa-tient, and accurate description of the data in which one spies principles. It is likewise for the steps in the demonstrations from which the conclusions follow. As a philosophy, Thomism has no other way for a true and authentic dissemination of itself. It is exemplified by the plethora of argumentation produced by Aquinas in the first three books of his *Summa Contra Gentiles*. For all his conviction that he was right and the "Gentiles" wrong, Aquinas knew that only rational discourse could make them see what he thought he understood.

Finally, one can also argue that the stunning display of philosophical reasoning in the *Summa Contra Gentiles* is still only a pale imitation of what to expect of a Thomist philosopher. Since, in these books, Aquinas is writing philosophy as a theologian, one can expect even more from a follower writing philosophy as a philosopher. In one's dialogue with other philosophers, one should never settle for cheap rhetorical tricks that only lead to the manipulation of others. Rather, with genuine care for the intellection of being in one's fellow, one must honestly and directly address the demands of natural reason. Honestly addressing these demands of true philosophical dialogue illustrates tolerant behavior.

3. True and False Diversity

Third, the appreciation of our fellows as intellectors of being also prepares us to acknowledge that the way in which one is genuinely respectful of one's fellows will vary analogically in different times and places. Being a good father in the Pacific islands will mean being a fisherman, while being a good father in Siberia will mean being a hunter. A respectful and solicitous treatment of our fellows as called for by their status as intellectors of being causes to burst forth an array of different behaviors that are genuinely expressive of the meaning of good father. And it is worth emphasizing that we will never witness the end of this array. In short, "good father" is what the Scholastics called an analogon. The earlier nongeneric intelligibility of being was another example of an analogon. The instances or data in whose differences the intellect spies the analogon the Scholastics called analogates.[7]

Some analogons are distinctive. These distinctive analogons have everything as their analogates. They are called transcendentals. The notion of being is a transcendental; it runs through the differences not only of all real things but also through cognitional items such as concepts, propositions, and syllogisms.[8] The notion of good father is an analogon that nevertheless is not a transcendental. Even though it can make its way into striking differences, not all differences can carry it. And so, not all instances are examples of good father, even among humans. But we should expect the notion of good father, as an analogon, to be realized in many different ways, all of which are genuine. One would be wrong to stereotype the analogon of good father by freezing it in terms of one or some of its analogates. The point here is more generally expressed by saying that one cannot stereotype the good or moral life. Being respectful toward one's fellows will lead to an analogical array of behaviors, each of which is legitimate. One clearly sees that differing does not always mean disagreeing.

Fidelity to our fellows as intellectors of being unleashes a creativity that is indicative of the richness of the notion of being itself. With a little philosophical imagination, one can see that such fidelity generates not only analogates of the analogon of good father but analogates of great teacher, good leader, excellent musician and artist, brave soldier, and so on. Here, fidelity to the transcendental of being present in the intellection of one's fellows generates truly novel instances that themselves are analogates of novel analogons. Analogate feeds on analogate.

But if Aquinas' notion of being provides inspiration for novelty, it also provides direction. Anticipating difference in the human realization of goodness does not mean that we can expect that anything goes at some time or other. For example, it does not mean that, at some time, it could be morally good to intend deliberately to kill the innocent or to deliberately commit adultery. Such actions will always be morally wrong because of the necessary blatant disrespect of the good present in the innocent or in one's spouse. This last point means that the creativity and intelligence—in short, the authenticity—that many postmodern philosophers want to use to characterize the moral life does not exclude absolute prohibitions. As noted, the analogous character of the moral good is compatible with these prohibitions. One does not have to trade the latter for the former as is done in much postmodern thinking.

In sum, consider how the saints exhibit Christian holiness in an analogical array. Each saint is holy but in a wild and crazily different way. We have the contemplatives, the martyrs, the scholars, the mendicants, the preachers, the missionaries, and so on. And who will be so foolish as to say that we have seen the end of this parade of saints? In the fourth century, one would have already seen an Augustine, a Basil, a Stephen, and a Paul. But one would not yet have witnessed the further analogates of sanctity to be realized in Francis, Aquinas, and Teresa.

Today, we are probably in the same position as someone in the fourth century. To the embarrassment of some Churchmen, the analogon of sanctity buries those who would stereotype and freeze it. Sanctity continually bursts its past forms. Nevertheless, notice how this great manifestation of human creativity is manifested within a context of absolute prohibitions. No saint as a saint is a liar, a murderer, a thief, or an adulterer. I think that we can say what a saint is not, but we can never claim to say what a saint is. So, just as Churchmen need to practice tolerance with those striving for sanctity, we all need to practice tolerance with our fellow members in society who are striving to live the moral life.

Finally, some reflection of this legitimate and noncontradictory pluralism exists in the speculative area. This legitimate pluralism must be kept distinct from a more popular form attributed to Aquinas. During the twentieth century, some Thomists attempted to construe Aquinas as a pluralist in philosophy. Being a pluralist meant that Aquinas did not and would not espouse in metaphysics a single conceptual expression of reality. Rather, any conceptual attempt to express reality would fall short and so, in principle, would leave room for another such attempt. For example, Aquinas defined basic act in terms of *esse*; an Augustinian would do the same in terms of *forma*. Since, for pluralists, Aquinas would regard his own definition as provisional, then Aquinas would have no decisive objection to understanding actuality basically in terms of having form.

Cited reasons for claiming a pluralist Aquinas include the following. First, concepts are abstractions, but abstractions leave something out about reality. Hence, even in its most fully developed concepts, the intellect's reach for reality falls short. Even when the intellect is conceiving a portion of reality, the abstractive nature of conception necessarily entails that that portion is only partly known. As an abstraction, that is, as something that leaves something out, any concept necessarily only approximates the real. Obviously, this fact, if true, leaves room for other approximations of the real, and so philosophical pluralism results.

Second, for Aquinas there exists an equivalency of being and of the true. But being is purely and simply in God and deficiently and imitatively in creatures. Hence, the true should be likewise. At best, creaturely truth is a deficient and never equaling imitation of divine truth. Just as no created being can claim to be the representation of being as such, so too no speculative system can claim to be the expression of truth as such.

Third, the Thomist pluralist claims that a basic a priori epistemology of intellectual dynamism exists in Aquinas. Just as, for Aquinas, something is a being only in and through a relation to Pure Existence, so too human truth should imply a relation to God. This relation is the tendency of the human spirit to the Absolute. Accordingly, the basic contact of human knowing with reality is found in its tendency to the Absolute. Truth is apportioned to other things in and through their relation to that dynamism. Since the mind's contact with Reality is supra-conceptual, an impassible divide exists between even the clearest and best built human system of thought and Truth itself. The best human system will never be the best system possible. In the wake of this epistemology, no absolute system, no unique system can exist. Hence, the Thomist synthesis exists side by side with that of Bonaventure, Duns Scotus, and Suarez as complementing rather than opposing positions. All these systems and future ones are part of the asymptotic effort of humans to reach the Absolute.

None of these three reasons for a conceptual-pluralist Aquinas succeed. The first reason leaves unacknowledged Aquinas' *De Ente et Essentia* distinction between abstraction with and abstraction without precision.[9] The first reason proceeds only in the light of the former type. Characteristic of precisive abstraction is that the attained commonality excludes what it does not include. As such, the commonality loses its identity with the datum and sinks to the level of a mere part of the datum. Humanity (*humanitas*) is a product of such precision. So, though we can say that Tom has humanity, we cannot say that Tom is humanity. But in abstraction without precision, the essence does not exclude what it does not include, and so predication, understood as an identification of whole and whole, can be preserved. We are not limited to saying Tom has humanity, but we can say that Tom *is* a human. In sum, nonprecisive abstraction keeps abstraction a fit instrument for dealing with reality.

With nonprecisive abstraction, you do decisively know the whole, albeit in a certain respect. On the other hand, with precisive abstraction, you can never say that you attain the whole. If abstraction is always precisive, then necessarily any one concept is going to leave something behind for another concept. It will do no good to say that what one concept leaves out another concept includes so that together both concepts are an expression of reality. The problem is that if all concepts are precisive, then the mega-concept formed by the other two must be precisive also. The mega-concept will, then, leave something out. This lack will leave room for another mega-concept. The inability of precisive concepts to grasp the whole, even from a perspective, is what creates the pluralism, just as the above first reason states. But the first reason is myopic about abstraction in Aquinas. Nonprecisive abstraction and its implications are unconsidered.

The second reason ignores that Aquinas understands the transcendental notion of being, the *ratio entis*, as an *analogous* abstraction without precision. As analogous, the notion of being is a sameness-in-difference. Hence, we intelligibly see it, but we see it through the differences of things that are its analogates. In short, we see it dimly and imperfectly. If we could, we would like to gaze upon the analogon itself. But unfortunately in this life, we are condemned to know more of being by knowing more of its analogates. This situation of our metaphysical knowledge in no way rivals the creator's perfect knowledge of the notion of being even while it includes the certainty that the basic description of the notion of being is *habens esse*.

Finally, the textual case for an epistemology of intellectual dynamism is weak. This is neither the time nor the place to go over the litany of Thomistic texts supposedly supportive of a basic a priori epistemology of intellectual dynamism in Aquinas.[10] Suffice it to say that in the light of the notion of being understood as an *abstractum*, intellectual dynamism appears to be an a posteriori phenomenon. Dynamism does not precede the concept here but follows it. We want to know more of the richness of being by knowing more beings. As mentioned, before one ever saw a platypus, could one have suspected that being could take the form of that animal? Does not that surprise ignite a desire to find out what else is out there?

But there exists another form of pluralism that is compatible with the one true metaphysics. This pluralism is exemplified by the number of arguments found in Aquinas' *Summa Contra Gentiles* versus the number of arguments in the *Summa Theologiae*. For example, if you had only read the *Summa Theologiae*, you could well come away thinking that the arguments for knowledge in God were just one in number. But if you turned to the *Summa Contra Gentiles* on the same point, you would see that Aquinas multiplies the arguments sevenfold. Aquinas has not changed metaphysics, but he has illustrated that there are many more ways to do the same thing.

My point is this. Who is to say that the *Summa Contra Gentiles* exhausts the possible arguments? After being embarrassed by the *Summa Contra Gentiles*, I do not think our reader of the *Summa Theologiae* would want to speak up. This reflection shows that Aquinas' one true metaphysics does not render us repeaters of a script. True, his metaphysics provides direction but not with a loss of inspiration. Within Aquinas' metaphysical context, there should always be more ways to say the same thing. No one should be dismissed simply on the grounds that his argument for knowledge in God is not recognizable as the one argument of the *Summa Theologiae*.

4. Heidegger on Being and Freedom

Even though, for Aquinas, human intellection is passive and receptive, the a posteriori character of intellection does not render us robots of the real, nor does it render us somehow unfaithful to ourselves and to the realization of our unique personalities. Such was the twentieth-century existentialist criticism of traditional philosophical thinking, especially as they said it culminated in Hegel. One existentialist who is especially appropriate to mention because of his lengthy disquisitions on the being of beings is the early Martin Heidegger. Hence, I would like to spend some time detailing Heidegger's position and comparing it to Aquinas'.

In *The Basic Problems of Phenomenology*, a work that was originally a series of lectures contemporary with *Being and Time* (1927),[11] Heidegger understands being as an a priori condition for the presencing of things. Many texts to this effect exist. I would like to quote at length one of the most striking of these. In detailing what he means by *being*, in the ontological difference between being and beings, Heidegger says,

> We are able to grasp beings as such, as being, only if we understand something like *being*. If we did not understand, even though at first roughly and without conceptual comprehension, what actuality signifies, then the actual would remain hidden from us. If we did not understand what reality means, then the real would remain inaccessible. . . . We must understand being so that we may be able to be given over to a world that is, so that we can exist in it and be our own *Dasein* itself as a being. We must be able to understand actuality before all experience of actual beings. This understanding of actuality or of being in the widest sense as over against the experience of beings is in a certain sense earlier than the experience of beings. To say that the understanding of being precedes all factual experience of beings does not mean that we would first need to have an explicit concept of being in order to experience beings theoretically or practically. We must understand being—being, which may no longer itself be called a being, being, which does not occur as a being among other beings but which nevertheless must be given and in fact is given in the understanding of being.[12]

What is the early Heidegger saying about being? As I understand him, he is saying that being is the expanse up and against which realities are seen as realities. The driving idea is that the individual is only known in the light of the universal. Undergirding this driving thought is Heidegger's description of what we experience. Does not saying that we experience beings mean that the beings are appreciated as instances of something larger—namely, being? Similarly, to experience Fido as a dog means to experience Fido as an instance of dog. But unlike dog, being is not derived from the beings that we experience. How could it be derived? Being sets up experienced beings in the first place.

Whenever we have beings, we already have being. Hence, in the previous quote, Heidegger says that being is "before" all experience of actual beings and that the understanding of being is "in a sense earlier than the experience of beings." Continuing this a priori construal of being, *Basic Problems* says that "the understanding of being has itself the mode of being of the human *Dasein*."

But if, for Heidegger, the being of beings is an a priori, it is not an a priori in the line of Kant's stable and immutable categorical structures of the mind. Later, in *Basic Problems*, Heidegger locates the general sense of being in what he calls *existential understanding*.[13] What is existential understanding? Heidegger calls it *verstehen* and equates it with the very existence of *Dasein*: "To be one's own most peculiar ability to be, to take it over and keep oneself in the possibility, to understand oneself in one's own factual freedom, that is, to understand oneself in the being of one's own most peculiar ability-to-be, is the original existential concept of understanding."[14]

As a basic determination of existence, understanding means our freedom, our being in control of, at the head of, and as such the meaning goes back to the etymology of the German *verstehen*—to stand in front of, at the head of, to preside over. Heidegger identifies understanding in the sense of freedom with the condition of possibility for all of *Dasein*'s particular manners of comportment, not only practical but also cognitive.[15]

This last remark, along with others,[16] is important because the remark seems to exclude a rational basis for freedom. But the absolute and underived character of understanding/freedom also comes out in Heidegger's clarification of the structure of understanding. In a word, understanding is projection.[17] Yet what I project upon is a can-be of my own self and what I project is my own self. These remarks confirm that understanding is self-contained. Nor should one think that the self contains some stable nature that controls or guides the exercise of freedom. Heidegger says that *Dasein* "is always only that which it has chosen itself to be, that which it understands itself to be in the projection of its own most peculiar ability-to-be."[18]

Heidegger goes on to insist, however, that understanding is not so self-contained as to involve an "isolated punctual ego."[19] *Dasein* is being-in-the-world. But again, the exercise of freedom remains what is prior so that intra-worldly being, including other *Dasein*s, are taken up in the light of that free projection. He says, "Along with understanding, there is always already projected a particular possible being with others and a particular possible being toward intra-worldly beings."[20] This talk of being in the world and being with others does not mean that *Dasein* ceases to be in the driver's seat. Heidegger says that authentic understanding consists in being determined primarily by oneself, not by things, circumstances, or others.[21]

In contrast, with inauthentic understanding, the awareness of *Dasein*'s freedom is lost. Hence, the future of inauthentic understanding is determined by the possibilities of things, not by the can-be of *Dasein*. Heidegger's way of saying it is this: "*Dasein* comes toward itself from out of things."[22] For the most part, *Dasein* exists in the temporality of inauthentic understanding. Inauthenticity predominates because *Dasein*'s intentionality first bears upon things in themselves.[23] Such a focus inadvertently covers over the founding role for things as played by *Dasein*.

So, for Heidegger, being is an a priori projection of *Dasein*'s freedom. And since being sets up things, and even the understanding of ourselves, *Dasein*'s freedom appears to be ungrounded. As noted, Heidegger insists that to take our possibilities from things is inauthentic *verstehen*. To live in the exercise of such freedom is "resoluteness" and is reserved for the few, the genuine philosophers and poets.[24] By placing freedom before what he means by being, Heidegger distinguishes his transcendental philosophy from Kant's. For Heidegger, the a priori projection of being is not the imposition of a stable and invariant category, as the a priori is for Kant. Also, by placing freedom before being, Heidegger's view certainly aggrandizes creativity and accommodates novelty. The obvious problem here is that on Heidegger's account the new and novel can be the bad and ugly. For example, there has never been a war like World War II.

As noted earlier, in Aquinas, being grounds freedom instead of freedom grounding a sense of being. Why the difference between these two thinkers? The answer is that the two are not speaking about the same thing. What Heidegger calls being is in truth what Aquinas regards as an analogate thereof. Hence, Heidegger describes being as a "world view" of which there can be many.[25] What Aquinas calls being is the transcendental analogon encompassing all these analogates. Heidegger appears to have no sense of what catches the attention of Aquinas. In his *Basic Problems* discussion of the medieval sense of being, which includes Aquinas, Heidegger repeatedly describes the *ratio entis*, which is called by Heidegger the *conceptus objectivus entis*, as the "emptiest" concept.[26]

This denomination of being as the emptiest shows that Heidegger understands being univocally. It also shows that Heidegger has no grasp of the analogous notion of being that is the central theme of Aquinas' philosophical reflections. Or perhaps said better, and by taking advantage of the distinction—made in the first section of chapter II above—between levels of self-evidence, it shows that Heidegger has no "explicit" knowledge of what Aquinas means by the *ratio entis*, but Heidegger knows it. Aquinas' *ratio entis* is in truth the "intelligible" space into which Heideggerian freedom flings the various senses of what Heidegger calls being. In other words, if, as Heidegger says, beings need being for their objectification, then what is the backdrop against which various senses of being are profiled? Aquinas' transcendental *abstractum* of being is there to answer that question.

Moreover, the novelty and creativity that Heidegger is rightfully concerned to safeguard is also accommodated by Aquinas' perspective. For before they ever saw any, who could suspect that being would express itself as a giraffe, a platypus, even something as mundane as grass and rock. The emergence of the analogates from the analogon of being is a veritable lesson in novelty. Hence, it is not surprising that poets and artists would want to do the same, even if they have no explicit understanding of analogons and analogates. Heidegger, in my opinion, is also smitten by the creativity of being. Unfortunately, he does not know how to express it.

The negative moral norms that arise in fidelity to being are important for the personal lives of artists also. If being teaches novelty, how can the artist be insensitive to being's heightened presence in the human? What teaches the artist art is preeminently in his fellows. Hence, it is a false dilemma to violate a person for the sake of art, as Frank Lloyd Wright did when he left his wife and family to pursue his architectural inspirations. Just as one cannot be morally good or spiritually holy and be a liar or a thief, so too one cannot be an artist and unfaithful to persons. What is the beauty of a building compared to the beauty of a person? Yes, art bows before being, but being is most intense in persons. Hence, if being is the beautiful and if being has its norms, then the beautiful does also. Ethics is for everyman, even the artists. The search for new experiences to evolve novel forms of the beautiful should never take the forms of infidelity, promiscuity, sadism, masochism, or self-abuse. By acknowledging these norms, the artist is not hindering a pursuit of the beautiful. Rather, the artist is expressing the deepest fidelity to the source of his inspiration—being as the beautiful both in the artist and in his fellows.[27]

NOTES:

[1] "The proof that the state is a creation of nature and prior to the individual is that the individual, when isolated, is not self-sufficing; and therefore he is like a part in relation to the whole. But he who is unable to live in society, or who has no need because he is sufficient for himself, must be either a beast or a god: he is no part of the state." Aristotle, *Politica* I, 2, 1253a 25–29; trans. by Benjamin Jowett in Richard McKeon's ed., *The Basic Works of Aristotle* (New York: Random House, 1941), 1130.

[2] "Therefore since [the earliest philosophers] philosophized in order to escape from ignorance, evidently they were pursuing science in order to know, and not for any utilitarian end. And this is confirmed by the facts; for it was when almost all the necessities of life and the things that make for comfort and recreation had been secured, that such knowledge began to be sought. Evidently then we do not seek it for the sake of any other advantage." Aristotle, *Metaphysics* I, 2, 982b 20–25; W. D. Ross trans., in McKeon, ed., *Basic Works*, 692. The trajectory of society to truth is reiterated by Aquinas in this observation: "In fact, all other human operations seem to be ordered to this one, as to an end. For, there is needed for the perfection of contemplation a soundness of body, to which all the products of art that are necessary for life are directed. Also required are freedom from the disturbances of the passions—this is achieved through the moral virtues and prudence—and freedom from external disorders, to which the whole program of government in civil life is directed. And so, if they are rightly considered, all human functions may be seen to subserve the contemplation of truth." Aquinas, *Summa Contra Gentiles* III, 37, *Ad hanc etiam omnes;* Bourke, trans., *Summa Contra Gentiles* III, pt. 1, 124.

[3] The external observation was extensively employed by John Henry Cardinal Newman in his *The Idea of a University* V, 3, though Cicero is the Ancient mentioned. Newman concludes, "Things, which can bear to be cut off from every thing else and yet persist in living, must have life in themselves; pursuits, which issue in nothing, and still maintain their ground for ages, which are regarded as admirable, though they have not as yet proved themselves to be useful, must have their sufficient end in themselves, whatever it turn out to be." *The Idea of a University* V, 4; as edited by Martin J. Svaglic (Notre Dame, IN: University of Notre Dame Press, 1982), 80.

[4] See *infra*, chapter VI, section 4, subsection b: *Dawson on world religions.*

[5] In my opinion, then, Rorty quits conversation too early: "Accommodation and tolerance must stop short of a willingness to work within any vocabulary that one's interlocutor wishes to use, to take seriously any topic that he puts forward for discussion. To take this view is of a piece with dropping the idea that a single moral vocabulary and a single set of moral beliefs are appropriate for every human community everywhere, and to grant that historical developments may lead us to simply drop questions and the vocabulary in which those questions are posed." "The Priority of Democracy to Philosophy," in *Objectivity, Relativism, and Truth* (Cambridge: Cambridge University Press, 1991), 190. The Thomistic opening with Rorty is to be found in discussing the basis for his claim that "persuasion" is

"analytic to [the] . . . meaning of 'better.'" "Cosmopolitanism without Emancipation" in *Objectivity, Relativism, and Truth*, p. 220.

⁶ Hence, Aquinas responds to a citation from Aristotle, "Evil is in many, but good is in few," that "The Philosopher is speaking with regard to men, in whom evil comes to pass from seeking after sensible pleasures, which are known to most men, and from forsaking the good dictated by reason, which good is known to few. In the angels there is only an intellectual nature, and hence the argument does not hold." *Summa Theologiae* I, 63, 9, ad 1m; ed. by Anton C. Pegis, *The Basic Writings of Saint Thomas Aquinas* (New York: Random House, 1945) vol. I, p. 599.

⁷ On the terminology of *analogon* and *analogate*, see George P. Klubertanz, *St. Thomas Aquinas on Analogy* (Chicago, IL: Loyola University Press, 1960), 6–7.

⁸ "We must realize (with the Philosopher) that the term 'a being' in itself has two meanings. Taken one way it is divided by the ten categories; taken in the other way it signifies the truth of propositions. The difference between the two is that in the second sense anything can be called a being if an affirmative proposition can be formed about it, even though it is nothing positive in reality." Aquinas, *De Ente et Essentia*, ch. 1; trans. by Armand A. Maurer, *On Being and Essence* (Toronto: Pontifical Institute of Mediaeval Studies, 1968), 29–30.

⁹ For the texts and a commentary, see Knasas, *Being and Some Twentieth-Century Thomists*, 39–42.

¹⁰ For a listing and critical analysis, see ibid., 45–61 and 95–128.

¹¹ Martin Heidegger, *The Basic Problems of Phenomenology*, trans. by Albert Hofstadter (Bloomington: Indiana University Press, 1988). The book is the text of a course that Heidegger gave at the University of Marburg in the summer of 1927. It was published only in 1975. Its close philosophical relationship to *Being and Time* is explained by Hofstadter in his "Translator's Introduction."

¹² Martin Heidegger, *The Basic Problems of Phenomenology*, 10–11. Also, see *Being and Time*, trans. John Macquarie and Edward Robinson (New York: Harper & Row, 1962): "Inquiry, as a kind of seeking, must be guided beforehand by what is sought. So the meaning of Being must already be available to us in some way" (pp. 25–26); "But as an investigation of Being, [phenomenological interpretation] brings to completion, autonomously and explicitly, that understanding of Being which belongs already to *Dasein* and which 'comes alive' in any of its dealings with entities" (p. 96); "understanding of Being has already been taken for granted in projecting upon possibilities. In projection, Being is understood, though not ontologically conceived. An entity whose kind of Being is the essential projection of Being-in-the-world has understanding of Being, and has this as constitutive of its Being" (pp. 187–188); "If what the term 'idealism' says, amounts to the understanding that Being can never be explained by entities but is already that which is 'transcendental' for every entity, then idealism affords the only correct possibility for a philosophical problematic" (p. 251). "At the bottom, however, the whole correlation necessarily gets thought of as somehow *being*, and must therefore be thought of with regard to some definite idea of Being" (p. 252); "[Common sense] fails to recognize that entities can be experienced 'factually' only when Being is already understood, even if it has not been conceptualized" (p. 363); "All ontical experience of entities—both circumspective calculation of the ready-to-hand, and positive scientific cognition of the present-at-hand—is based upon projections of the Being of the corresponding entities" (p. 371); "[the paradigmatic character of mathematical natural science] consists rather in the fact that the entities which it takes as its theme are discovered in it in the only way in which entities can be discovered—by the prior projection of their state of Being" (p. 414). In sum, John Caputo, *Heidegger and Aquinas: An Essay*

on Overcoming Metaphysics (New York: Fordham University Press, 1982), 53, remarks, "[In *Being and Time,*] Being is the meaning or horizon of understanding within which beings are manifest. Thus instead of being an abstract concept, a vacuous abstraction when separated from concrete beings, ... Being for Heidegger becomes the meaning-giving horizon, the transcendental *a priori*, which precedes beings and renders them possible in their Being. It is not an abstraction drawn from beings, but an *a priori* which precedes them."

[13] "An understanding of the being of existence in general is enclosed in every existential understanding." Heidegger, *Basic Problems*, 279.

[14] Ibid., 276.

[15] "If understanding is the basic determination of existence, it is as such the condition of possibility for all of *Dasein's* particular possible manners of comportment. It is the condition of possibility for all kinds of comportment, not only practical but also cognitive." Ibid.

[16] "If, however, an understanding of being always already lies at the basis of all comportment of the *Dasein* toward beings, whether nature or history, whether theoretical or practical, then plainly I cannot adequately define the concept of understanding if, in trying to make the definition, I look solely to specific types of cognitive comportment towards beings. Thus what is required is to find a sufficiently original concept of understanding from which alone not only all modes of cognition but every type of comportment that relates to beings by inspection and circumspection can be conceived in a fundamental way." Ibid., 275.

[17] "To understand means, more precisely, *to project oneself upon a possibility.*" Ibid., 277.

[18] Ibid., 278.

[19] Ibid.

[20] Ibid.

[21] "[*Dasein*] can let its existence be determined primarily not by itself but by things and circumstances and by the others. It is the understanding that we call inauthentic understanding. . . . ['Inauthentic'] denotes an understanding in which the existent *Dasein* does not understand itself primarily by the apprehended possibility of itself which is most peculiarly its own." Ibid., 279. Heidegger's notion of *verstehen* strikingly calls to mind Sartre's position on the absolute freedom of the human subject, the *pour-soi*. In *Being and Nothingness*, trans. by Hazel E. Barnes (New York: Washington Square, 1969), Sartre passionately argues that we are not limited by our place, past, surroundings, fellow-brethren, or death. In general, Sartre points out that the coefficient of adversity found in these items is always a factor of our freely chosen projects. The standard example is the boulder on the road (ibid., 620). What it is—a help or a hindrance—depends upon what I want to do. If I wish to travel to a town beyond, the boulder is a hindrance; if I wish to survey the countryside, the boulder becomes a help. It is true that in his *Letter on Humanism*, edited by David Farrell Knell, *Martin Heidegger: Basic Writings* (New York: Harper & Row, 1977), 208, Heidegger takes some pains to distinguish his position from Sartrean existentialism. To Heidegger's mind, Sartre is still too metaphysical—specifically, he is insufficiently attentive to the being of beings. Sartrean projection is upon already present beings and so aligns itself with a subjectivity that exploits and manipulates beings. Heidegger wants to avoid this subjectivity by a more radical subjectivity that accounts for the very being in the light of which beings themselves become present. From my perspective, this dispute Heidegger picks with Sartrean existentialism is a lover's quarrel, for common to both is the primacy of the play of projection. Even though Heidegger insists that "man does not decide whether and how

beings appear . . . the advent of beings lies in the destiny of Being" (*Letter on Humanism*, 210), and also remarks that "the sentence [from *Being and Time*: 'Only so long as *Dasein* is, is there Being.'] does not say that Being is the product of man," (ibid., 216) the term *man* here does not mean Heideggerian *Dasein*. Rather, *man* means "the *Dasein* of man in the traditional sense of *existentia* and thought in modern philosophy as the actuality of *ego cogito*." Already cited texts from *Basic Problems* indicate quite unmistakably that Heideggerian *Dasein* does decide how beings appear and does produce the being of beings, even if Sartre's Cartesian *Dasein* does not.

²² Heidegger, *Basic Problems*, 289.

²³ For Heidegger's analysis of perceptual intentionality and the projection of being contained within it, see ibid., 55–72. *Basic Problems* does contain some apparently realist assertions. First, Heidegger insists (p. 49) that a window "does not receive existence from my perceiving, but just the reverse. I can perceive it only if it exists and because it exists. . . . Perception or absolute position is at most the mode of access to the existent." Second, he says that "perceivedness is not equated with extantness but is only a necessary though indeed not a sufficient condition of access to extantness" (p. 67). But realism is not the sure interpretation here. To the first text, one could say that perceiving does not give the window existence because the projecting of being does that. As Heidegger says (p. 52), "Being is what makes a being what it is as a being." In the same vein, one can read Heidegger's *Being and Time* remark: "Entities *are*, quite independently of the experience by which they are disclosed" (p. 228). To the second text, one could say that the necessary further condition for perception is not only the extantness of the perceived but *Dasein*'s projection of being. In *Basic Problems*, Heidegger does say "with respect to its possibility, perceivedness is grounded in the understanding of extantness" (p. 71).

²⁴ "Philosophy is always the concern of the few. Which few? The creators, those who initiate profound transformations. It spreads only indirectly, by devious paths that can never be laid out in advance, until at last, at some future date, it sinks to the level of a commonplace; but by then it has long been forgotten as original philosophy. What philosophy essentially can and must be is this: a thinking that breaks the paths and opens the perspectives of the knowledge that sets the norms and hierarchies, of knowledge in which and by which a people fulfills itself historically and culturally, the knowledge that kindles and necessitates all inquiries and thereby threatens all values." Martin Heidegger, *Introduction to Metaphysics*, trans. by Ralph Manheim (New Haven, CT: Yale University Press, 1977), 10. 37. For poets, Heidegger singles out Hölderlin because Hölderlin wrote expressly of the essence of poetry. What Hölderlin reveals, Heidegger describes this way: "The poet names the gods and names all things in that which they are. This naming does not consist merely in something already known being supplied with a name; it is rather that when the poet speaks the essential word, the existent is by this naming nominated as what it is. So it becomes known *as* existent. Poetry is the establishing of being by means of the word. . . . But because being and essence of things can never be calculated and derived from what is present, they must be freely created, laid down and given. Such a free act of giving is establishment." Martin Heidegger, "Hölderlin and the Essence of Poetry" edited by Werner Brock, *Martin Heidegger: Existence and Being* (Chicago, IL: Henry Regnery, 1968), 281. On the other hand, Sartre appears to democratize the freedom that Heidegger gives only to the few: "Thus, the first effect of existentialism is that it puts every man in possession of himself as he is, and places the entire responsibility for his existence squarely upon his own shoulders." Jean-Paul Sartre, *Existentialism and Humanism*, trans. by Philip Mairet (London: Methuen, 1948), 29. See also Sartre's discussion of apparent obstacles to our freedom in *Being and*

Nothingness, pt. 4, ch. 1. Despite his preference for liberal democracy, Richard Rorty appears to opt for the more elitist line of Heidegger: "For if we use the former vocabulary [Dewey's, Heidegger's, Davidson's, and Derrida's], we shall be able to see moral progress as a history of making rather than finding, of poetic achievement by 'radically situated' individuals and communities, rather than as the gradual unveiling, through the use of 'reason,' of 'principles' or 'rights' or 'values.'" "The Priority of Democracy to Philosophy," 189. Also, "The liberal response to the communitarians' second claim must be, therefore, that even if the typical character types of liberal democracies *are* bland, calculating, petty, and unheroic, the prevalence of such people may be a reasonable price to pay for political freedom." Ibid., 190.

[25] Heidegger, *Basic Problems*, 296–297.

[26] "In the view of Scholasticism and of philosophy in general, this concept of being is the *ratio abstractissima et simplicissima*, the emptiest and simplest concept, the one that is most undetermined and simple, the immediate. . . . No definition is possible of this most universal and empty concept [*ratio entis*]." Heidegger, *Basic Problems*, 84.

[27] In his excellent *Art and Scholasticism* (London: Sheed & Ward, 1946), 106, Jacques Maritain incisively notes, "Only the artist who consents to be a man, who is not afraid of morality, who is not every moment terrified of losing the flower of his ingenuousness, enjoys the real gratuitousness of art. He is what he is, careless of what he may appear to be; he affirms if he wants to affirm, he believes, loves, chooses, gives himself, follows his inclination and his fancy, recreates and amuses himself, enjoys himself playing."

V

DEFENDING TOLERANCE WITHOUT BECOMING INTOLERANT

So in these three ways—through establishing the good of society, by insisting on the propriety of dialogue, and by evincing the analogous character of moral living—Aquinas' ethical thinking makes a place for tolerance. But Aquinas' thinking is not so open that it relinquishes any logic for its own defense. Aquinas can defend tolerance without becoming intolerant himself. Those philosophies especially deserving of criticism are not those philosophies that disagree with mine but those philosophies that cannot logically accommodate the fraternal respect that is the basic component of the common good. Remember, this is a fact that all philosophies must accommodate. The twentieth century has taught us this. Hence, the common good is not an imposition of Thomism. Just as philosophers penalized, wrongly in my opinion, natural law ethics as too wedded to moral absolutes to ground the tolerance necessary for society, Aquinas can now turn the tables. Since Aquinas has logically accommodated not just tolerance in the usual sense but also tolerance in the sense of fraternal tolerance, Aquinas has a place a fortiori in the public discussion. The Thomist can now make the same demand of other philosophies. Again, it does no good to retreat into skepticism to defend tolerance. If no truth exists, then no way exists to prevent the emergence of someone, like Hitler, who thinks that might makes right.

1. Hedonism and Utilitarianism

First, how could society defend the tolerance component of the common good nonlegalistically? Through social pundits, philosophers, and the conversation of ordinary citizens, the proponents of philosophies unable to accommodate fraternal respect would be kept under critical scrutiny and logical ridicule. Until they explain how their philosophies accommodate tolerance , they should suffer the same lash that Thomists have suffered. The lifestyle results of these philosophies—such as pornography from hedonism—will not be supported by the citizenry. In rightful disgust, the citizenry will turn its back to them. For example, in the temperance movements of the nineteenth century, Eastern Europeans turned their backs to the slavery of Russian alcohol. In sum, a nation of virtue will leave the practical results of these philosophies to wither on the vine.

To illustrate how other philosophies fail to accommodate tolerance, let me go through the following list. Can a hedonist accommodate the mutual goodwill demanded by the common good? This accommodation is highly unlikely. By defining the good in terms of pleasure or the absence of pain, the hedonist, like Epicurus,[1] makes the good so subjective that any kind of genuine self-sacrifice for one's fellows looks ridiculous. That is the problem with the Hollywood of MTV. It is all about getting your own pleasure. I do not deny that rock stars can be involved in philanthropic activities—Bono of U2, for example—but I deny that these activities have any logical connection to hedonism. Just as a Thomist can fail to realize the social implications of his philosophy, so too, a hedonist can fail to stick with the egotistical implications of hedonism. In fact, that hedonists become altruistic and do not remain in the narrow circle of personal pleasure is some grudging admission of the truth (about the human person) in Thomism.

J. S. Mill's utilitarianism is no advance over this problem in hedonism. First, Mill equates happiness with pleasure which seems to mean a sensate experience. Pleasure's sensate nature becomes apparent in Mill's remarks on the inculcation of virtue:

> How can the will to be virtuous, where it does not exist in sufficient force, be implanted or awakened? Only by making the person *desire* virtue—by making him think of it in a pleasurable light, or of its absence in a painful one. It is by associating the doing right with pleasure, or the wrong with pain, or by eliciting and impressing and bringing home to the person's experience the pleasure naturally involved in the one or the pain in the other, that it is possible to call forth that will to be virtuous, which, when confirmed, acts without any thought of either pleasure or pain. Will is the child of desire, and passes out of the dominion of its parent only to come under that of habit.[2]

Scenes of spare the rod and spoil the child come to mind. Mill's proof that happiness is pleasure consists in an introspection that reveals that nothing is desired except because of its pleasure:

And now to decide whether this is really so, whether mankind do desire nothing for itself but that which is a pleasure to them, or of which the absence is a pain, we have evidently arrived at a question of fact and experience, dependent, like all similar questions, upon evidence. It can only be determined by practiced self-consciousness and self-observation, assisted by observation of others. I believe that these sources of evidence, impartially consulted, will declare that desiring a thing and finding it pleasant, aversion to it and thinking of it as painful, are phenomena entirely inseparable, or rather, two parts of the same phenomenon—in strictness of language, two different modes of naming the same psychological fact.[3]

Mill is so confident of his psychological observation that he declares, ". . . to desire anything, except in proportion as the idea of it is pleasant, is a physical and metaphysical impossibility."[4]

Second, according to Mill, among these sensate experiences called pleasure, some are of a better quality than others. For example, the pleasures of pursuing knowledge and of acting for others are better than the pleasures of eating and of sex.

But there is no known Epicurean theory of life which does not assign to the pleasures of the intellect, of the feelings and imagination, and of the moral sentiments, a much higher value as pleasures than to those of mere sensation. . . . It is quite compatible with the principle of utility to recognize the fact that some kinds of pleasure are more desirable and more valuable than others. It would be absurd that, while in estimating all other things quality is considered as well as quantity, the estimation of pleasures should be supposed to depend on quantity alone.[5]

As proof for this second point, Mill says that he can only appeal to the opinion of those who have a familiarity with both pleasures: "If one of the two [pleasures] is, by those who are competently acquainted with both, placed so far above the other that they prefer it, even though knowing it to be attended with a greater amount of discontent, and would not resign it for any quantity of the other pleasure which their nature is capable of, we are justified in ascribing to the preferred enjoyment a superiority in quality, so far outweighing quantity as to render it, in comparison, of small account."[6]

What does this appeal show? "Few human creatures would consent to be changed into any of the lower animals for a promise of the fullest allowance of a beast's pleasures; no intelligent human being would consent to be a fool, no instructed person would be an ignoramus, no person of feeling and conscience would be selfish and base, even though they should be persuaded that the fool, the dunce, or the rascal is better satisfied with his lot than they are with theirs."[7]

By way of comment, Mill should be commended for extolling the qualitative differences between pleasures. But the extolling may indicate an intrusion within Mill's sensate psychology. For what I find metaphysically impossible is Mill's attempt to accommodate altruism. Undoubtedly, a low-grade altruism is integrated into Mill's position. We all know of people who encourage others to be generous because they will feel good. But inconsistencies within the psychology develop when the altruism is heroic. In this case the hero knows that the altruism will cause the hero's death. The inconsistency is that someone who is supposedly always acting for his own pleasure is knowingly doing something that brings about his extinction and so his cessation of any and all pleasure. Mill admits the difficulty here and appears to modify his sensate psychology to deal with the difficulty. First, Mill says that the hero is at least acting for the happiness of others: ". . . [doing without happiness] often has to be done voluntarily by the hero or the martyr, for the sake of something which he prizes more than his individual happiness. But this something, what is it, unless the happiness of others, or some of the requisites of happiness?"[8]

But given his psychology, with the above-mentioned observed metaphysical necessity, what Mill should have said is that the hero acts for the pleasure that he feels in helping others. But there then follows my criticism that such action is ridiculous when the hero realizes that his action is, for him, pleasure-extinguishing. Interestingly, in the next paragraph Mill appears to concede that, in the case of the hero, his psychology of sensate pleasure will not work: "I will add that in this condition of the world, paradoxical as the assertion may be, the conscious ability to do without happiness gives the best prospect of realizing such happiness as is attainable."[9] But if it is metaphysically necessary to act for one's own pleasure, then the conscious ability to act for some other end is not just paradoxical but contradictory. In other words, where is my pleasure in doing knowingly something that will end all my pleasure?

Evidently, Mill lacks the appropriate psychology for his ethical project. Yet the pleasures that he selects as qualitatively superior and his lionizing the happiness of the greatest number suggest to a Thomist that operative in Mill is a different psychology than Mill's psychology of sensate pleasure. That implicit psychology would be that of Aquinas'—detailed in chapter II above. As noted, the first object of willing is the *ratio entis* understood as the *ratio boni*. This object of the will does not yet include ourselves, for as yet there is no reflection upon ourselves. That self-reflection occurs later and is important for the genesis of the moral obligation to treat ourselves with respect and solicitude. Our love of being as the good blossoms into a love of self insofar as being is appreciated as the object in our intellection. So, we love ourselves and our intellection in and through the presence of what we primarily love, namely, the notion of being. Again, the first object of the will is being. The notion of being is not something subjective. It is expressive of real things, and moreover it is a commonality intensely found in other humans. Love of others is engendered insofar as, like us, others have through their intellection the notion of being in an especially intense manner. In Aquinas' psychology, our most fundamental desire is first for being, then for our intellection of being, then for being in our fellows. Aquinas' psychology has a place for heroism because what we primarily love is something other than ourselves—the notion of being. Moreover, this notion has a greater presence in the multitude than in the individual, so it can quite understandably lead to a moral injunction of self-sacrifice for one's society.

True, in his discussion of happiness, or beatitude, at *Summa Theologiae* I–II, 1, 7c, Aquinas distinguishes two components in the notion of happiness: first, the thing in which the *ratio boni* is found and, second, the use or possession of that thing. For example, the end of the miser is not just money but the hoarding of money. Would not this model of happiness create for Aquinas the egotism problem that I have ascribed to Mill? It seems so. For our end would not be simply the notion of being but to unite with being by intellection and virtuous living. So, something proper to us is part of happiness. For example, the relation to being through virtuous living is extremely personal, for it occurs in and through our free choices that respect our fellows. Something of ourselves is a portion of the bull's-eye of happiness. How can I aim for happiness and not aim for myself?

As I asked Mill, a utilitarian can ask Aquinas if Aquinas' ethics can accommodate self-sacrifice to the heroic degree. In reply, the equivalency arises because the dynamism of Aquinas' philosophical psychology is forgotten. The portions of the above twofold notion of happiness are not portions of a static whole. As noted, happiness is something that is unfolded beginning with its objective portion—the notion of being. As the good, being itself is what claims our attention and desire. Other things are included in our attention insofar as they are appreciated as epiphanies, or heightened presentations, of being. These epiphanies include not simply our individual intellection or moral free choices but those of our fellows in society at large. Not only does the well-being of our own personal selves have a claim on us, but so too does the well-being of society. In fact the moral claim of the latter is greater because of the greater intensity of being in society at large. So, if we love being, we will especially be respectful and solicitous of the well-being of society which harbors being more intensely than an individual human.

In conclusion, because of the empiricist tradition of which Mill is a member, Mill is striving to root our ideas of obligation in experience. Mill's approach is fortuitous for it makes appropriate a confrontation of phenomenologies of human subjectivity. But the nominalism of the empiricist tradition hides from Mill's phenomonological study of human psychology the very thing that his ethical ideas need in order to be based upon human experience. The phenomenology must be more empirical without becoming empiricist. It must reveal the truly intellectual dimensions of human experience. A Thomist would invite the utilitarian to reconsider his subjectivity in the light of Aquinas' analyses and ask him to see if he has missed something. Aquinas' psychology can be so implicit that it escapes notice but nevertheless has conscious effects. One of these effects can be a deep love of our fellows. But because the psychology is so implicit, one can confuse the basis of that love and go on to locate that basis in something that fails to support it. Indications in Mill of an implicit Thomistic psychology are the intellectual and moral pleasures that Mill extolls as well as his espousal of the greatest happiness principle.

2. Kant's Ethics of Practical Reason

The problem with Kant's ethics is not that it denies brotherly love. The problem is that Kantian ethics does not logically imply it. For Kantian ethics to logically imply fraternity would admit a heteronomy that is anathema to the will's autonomy.[10] Hence, we are left irrationally hoping that autonomous wills just happen to opt for respectful tolerance.

In his *Groundwork for the Metaphysics of Morals*, Kant investigates the source for the appearance of moral necessity, or obligation. I summarize Kant's analysis as follows. Kant begins with the *good will*. The good will is the will that acts for the sake of the law alone and not for any benefit derived from following the law.[11] But what does fidelity to the law mean? It means fidelity to what characterizes law. And what is that? It is universality. A law makes universal claims: *no* one, nowhere, can do such and such.[12] Next, this fidelity to universality is articulated in terms of the categorical imperative: do only what you are able to universalize.[13] Somewhat similarly, we say in Christianity,"Love your neighbor as yourself." But Kant pushes the analysis further. Why the categorical imperative?

For Kant, the categorical imperative is grounded in the idea of a rational being as an end in itself.[14] How so? Well, reflect upon what violating the imperative means. If I am willing to say that the proscription of lying is not universal, then I am saying that in some circumstances I can be lied to. Now, for Kant there is something insulting about that thought. The insult is that I am being treated as a mere means to someone else's end. To Kant, that treatment is a striking violation of our dignity. Our dignity, then, is that we are ends unto ourselves.

But Kant's analysis continues. That we are ends means that we must regard ourselves as self-legislating.[15] Kant translates this idea of a self-legislator into the idea of the autonomous will.[16] Such a will is absolutely free in that it takes no cues for its exercise from anything else. In other words, not even knowledge of the moral law precedes the will. Such a reference for the will would encroach on the will's autonomy.[17]

If I have understood Kant, I wonder if his analysis cuts off the branch on which it is sitting. The analysis is supposed to explain the appearance of moral necessity, or obligation. But, in my opinion, the analysis concludes to a will so autonomous that it is not bound by anything, including the categorical imperative. I know that Kant acknowledges that the categorical imperative is the "supreme law" of a good will[18] and that the imperative is compatible with the will's autonomy.[19] Yet, I insist on an explanation.

Kant says that heteronomy exists when the will seeks the moral law in the character of its object. But is not the supreme law, the categorical imperative, a response to our character as ends unto ourselves? It seems so.[20] It does no good to reply that heteronomy only results when the will is related to the character of something *other* than itself. For the character of the will itself is in some sense other than the will insofar as the will is *of* such a character. In sum, the categorical imperative expresses to the will the marching orders of the character of the will. How is this situation compatible with Kant's talk about the autonomy of the will and talk of the will legislating its laws?

The will seems to be not autonomous in respect to its character, and its laws seem to be dictated not by itself but by the character-imposed categorical imperative. Hence, in my opinion, the only way that Kant can avoid inconsistency is to admit that the will is so autonomous that it self-legislates even the categorical imperative. And if self-legislation is the correct conclusion of Kant's logic, then what happens to moral necessity? Can a true creator of legislation be considered as genuinely bound by that legislation? Is not the idea of a self-legislator a contradiction in terms? In sum, what is arbitrarily asserted can always be arbitrarily denied, even by the original asserter. Hence, Kant brings the project of ethics to an impasse. Insofar as he explains obligation in a way that extinguishes obligation, then to preserve obligation we have to leave obligation unexplained. Ethics has lost its future.[21]

Aquinas also employs human freedom to evoke obligation. At *Summa Contra Gentiles* III, 112, Aquinas explains why in God's providence God governs rational creatures for their own sake, not in subordination to some other creature. Aquinas' thinking here is most relevant for human ethics because if God has to treat us in a particular way because we are free, then a fortiori, and for the same reason, we should treat each other similarly. Aquinas says,

> The very way in which the intellectual creature was made, according as it is master of its acts, demands providential care whereby this creature may provide for itself, on its own behalf; while the way in which other things were created, things which have no dominion over their acts, shows this fact, that they are cared for, not for their own sake, but as subordinated to others. That which is moved only by another being has the formal character of an instrument, but that which acts of itself has the essential character of a principal agent. Now, an instrument is not valued for its own sake, but as useful to a principal agent. Hence it must be that all the careful work that is devoted to instruments is actually done for the sake of the agent, as for an end, but what is done for the principal agent, either by himself or by another, is for his own sake, because he is the principal agent. Therefore, intellectual creatures are so controlled by God, as objects of care for their own sakes; while other creatures are subordinated, as it were, to the rational creatures.[22]

Aquinas uses the freedom of the rational creature to argue that it should be treated for its own sake. In other words, Aquinas grounds the dignity of the human on its freedom of will. In *Groundwork*, Kant argued in opposite fashion. He concludes to the autonomy of will from our being ends unto ourselves.[23] No conflict exists here because Kant is just proceeding analytically to what Aquinas uses as a starting point.[24] It remains for both that freedom is the principle of morals.

Yet each understands freedom differently. For Aquinas, the free agent is not a self-legislator but a self-determiner, an agent that acts through its own consent. Unlike Kant's autonomous will, which is incompatible with direction by reason, the freedom of a self-determiner is compatible with rational direction. In fact, Aquinas indicates the object of that direction in another argument of chapter 112:

> It is evident that all parts are ordered to the perfection of the whole, since a whole does not exist for the sake of its parts, but, rather, the parts are for the whole. Now intellectual natures have a closer relationship to a whole than do other natures; indeed, each intellectual substance is, in a way, all things. For it may comprehend the entirety of being through its intellect [*inquantum totius entis comprehensiva est suo intellectu*]; on the other hand, every other substance has only a particular share in being. Therefore, other substances may fittingly be providentially cared for by God for the sake of intellectual substances.[25]

The human as an intellector of being is what directs God's providence to govern the human for its own sake. This same understanding of ourselves and our fellows should be what merits the respect and solicitude of our free will.

To understand Aquinas' argument, two points are important. The notion of being, the *ratio entis*, is not just any whole or entirety. Being is a transcendental analogon. As such, it is a commonality, or intelligibility, that implicitly but actually contains the different perfections of all conceivable things. This thinking about being follows from Aquinas' repeated assertions that addition to being is not from outside as is the case with the addition of a species to a genus. Rather, addition to being is *via* the differences expressing what is actually but implicitly contained by the notion.[26] Hence, the *ratio entis* is not just any whole; it is the whole that contains the perfections of all things. In sum, the *ratio entis* is also the good, the *ratio boni*.

Second, following Aristotle, Aquinas views cognition, both sensory and intellectual, as an especially intimate becoming of the known by the knower. Knowers have an "amplitude" and an "extension" of form over matter that allows them to receive the very form of the thing known without detriment to themselves.[27] As so conformed to the known, the knower is suitably equipped to produce it as the term of the knower's cognitive activities.

These two points mean that in the human person—understood as what I call an "intellector of being"—we confront an especially intense presence of the good. It is no wonder that even God relates to the rational creature in a providence that governs the rational creature for its own sake. So, in Aquinas, freedom is guided freedom. Reason addresses freedom with facts that include moral necessity. Our fellows are intellectors of being and being is the good.

As I described in chapter II, these facts are crucial for understanding Aquinas' seminal article on the basis of natural law ethics in his *Summa Theologiae* I–II, 94, 2c. For Aquinas, the future of ethics lies in being faithful to these facts in all of our various activities. In contrast, for Kant, if I have understood him correctly, no facts can address our freedom. Any such address would compromise the autonomy of the will and Kant's understanding of the will as self-legislating.

In conclusion, both Kant and Aquinas ground human dignity upon human freedom. But both understand human freedom differently. For Kant, human freedom is self-legislating and so is exercised without rational direction. As noted, this human freedom shuts down the ethical project because the will is so autonomous that any legislating is only a charade. Moral necessity, or obligation, disappears. For Aquinas, human freedom is self-determining. By *self-determining* I mean acting from one's consent. The Thomistic notion of freedom is not only compatible with rational direction, it is also compatible with the phenomena that Kant analyzes for his purposes.

The latter point is important for noticing that Kant's analysis seems to commit a non sequitur. That I ought to be treated as an end does not strictly entail that I ought to be regarded as self-legislating. It suffices that I be thought of as self-determining. Such an agent is also an end. Your capacity for self-determination forces me to respect you for yourself and so as an end. The idea of being self-determining also explains the insult that we feel in being lied to. By the lie we are enlisted in a project for which we did not give our consent. So, Aquinas can take the best features of Kant's position—human dignity and its connection with human freedom—but parlay them so that they do not become antinomies. As self-determination, human freedom is still a ground for human dignity.

3. Rawls' Political Liberalism

Currently, I am arguing that among ethical theories only Aquinas' previously described natural law ethics accommodates the desideratum of fraternal tolerance. Some readers might see my present thesis as effecting a straw-man argument. Their reason could be that someone like the famous twentieth-century political philosopher John Rawls grounds tolerance apart from any ethical theory, or for that matter, apart from any philosophical or religious view. Hence, my rendering of Aquinas' natural law ethics through his metaphysics is a woefully over-complicated and divisive rendering of a much sought after value. So, I now turn to Rawls.

In his *Political Liberalism*, John Rawls connects the question of tolerance— how there can exist a stable society of citizens who are divided by religious, philosophical, and moral doctrines—with the issue of the most appropriate conception of justice for free and equal citizens over a complete life and from one generation to the next.[28] Hence, the answer to the second question applies to the first. The answer to the second question is the two principles of justice.[29] First, each person has an equal claim to the basic rights and liberties, and second, social and economic inequalities must attach to positions open to all and must rebound to the least advantaged. So, Rawls' accommodation of tolerance reduces to his grounding of the principles of justice.

I want to analyze Rawls' various ways of expressing this grounding. Rawls limits his explanations to grounding the basic liberties of freedom of thought and liberty of conscience and why the first principle of justice that expresses these liberties has priority over the second principle.[30] I will focus on the former.

As an introductory point, all of Rawls' explanations assume the mindset of the "original position." Characteristic of the original position is the wearing of a "veil of ignorance." In other words, one does not know how one will be in society. For example, one does not know if one will be rich or poor, religious or secularist, Kantian or utilitarian. In light of this ignorance, one assesses various proposed principles of justice. Rawls' claim is that his above two principles of justice will be selected by those in the original position. Hence, as expressed by the two principles, Rawls' political liberalism is a "freestanding" view.[31] Rawls' procedure is best understood by review of its usage for the two mentioned liberties.

The first example is explicitly about a basis for tolerance.[32] Here, persons enter the original position in the light of the "burdens of judgment."

The burdens of judgment are the various impediments that prevent reasonable people from coming to agreement about comprehensive views—namely, the mentioned religious, moral, and philosophical views. The burdens include these: conflicting and complex evidence, weight to be given agreed upon criteria, need for interpretation, disparate total experiences of citizens, and the need to choose values because of the incompatibility of values. Rawls contends that, with the burdens of judgment in mind, no reasonable person in the original position would consent ". . . to use state power, the collective power of equal citizens, to prevent the rest from affirming their not unreasonable views."[33] His argument for this conclusion is expressed as such:

> To confirm this conclusion, let us look at the case from another point of view and say: citizens as free and equal have an equal share in the corporate political and coercive power of society, and all are equally subject to the burdens of judgment. There is no reason, then, why any citizen, or association of citizens, should have the right to use the state's police power to decide constitutional essentials or basic questions of justice as that person's, or that association's, comprehensive doctrine directs. This can be expressed by saying that when equally represented in the original position, no citizen's representative could grant to any other person, or association of persons, the political authority to do that. Such authority is without grounds in public reason. What would be proposed instead is a form of toleration and freedom of thought consistent with the preceding reasoning.[34]

Rawls places his argument against some one group using state power against others in terms of the equality of the groups. Since the groups are equal, no one group has a reason to do this. Earlier, Rawls described his basis for the equality of groups: "The basic idea is that in virtue of their two moral powers (a capacity for a sense of justice and for a conception of the good) and the powers of reason (of judgment, thought, and inference connected with these powers), persons are free. Their having these powers to the requisite minimum degree to be fully cooperating members of society makes persons equal."[35]

One's agreement with Rawls' conclusion should not blind one to the fact that his first argument is unconvincing. First, if the argument does conclude, the argument concludes to more than tolerance and so is imperfect. To what else does the argument conclude? The argument also concludes to the equal right of the persons and their representatives to use state power or to fight to impose their view of the truth. The argument needs to exclude that implication.

Second, why is mere equality morally relevant? Two apples are equal. I smash one and eat the other. So *what* if I did not treat them equally? I may even decide not to treat them at all. Instead I consume oranges. Again, so *what*? Obviously, Rawls thinks that when the equals are humans, then there is something more. Humans are special equals. Humans are equals in dignity; humans have the highest value. I believe that this premise of human dignity is what constrains Rawls' first argument to conclude to tolerance and not to a free-for-all.

But how does Rawls establish the premise of human dignity? As noted, he sees equality in terms of freedom. Finally, behind freedom are the moral powers and the powers of reason. Does the dignity of the human person appear in this material? Maybe, maybe not. To my mind, the issue that must be clarified is the relation between these two powers. If we take seriously that Rawls always mentions the powers of reason after and second to the moral powers, then Rawls is still within the thinking of Kant on the autonomous will. This context would not only violate the norms of his original position but, as I explained in the previous section on Kant, it would more importantly fail to ground any moral norm. We would be left simply hoping that the autonomous will chooses to be tolerant. On the other hand, if the relation between the powers has the powers of reason guiding the moral powers, then how is this to be explained so that the obligatory value of human dignity is on the scene? Does not one have to return to the intellection of being as a precondition for human freedom? Does not one have to understand autonomy in terms of self-determination instead of self-legislation?

In sum, Rawls' first argument presupposes an intuition that his public reason cannot provide but without which his first argument cannot conclude. It presupposes that when it comes to humans, no fact/value distinction exists. Given the presence of disagreeing Humeans, Rawls appears to be imposing a comprehensive view. Rawls should admit that his political liberalism is not freestanding. It needs the truth of Aquinas' natural law ethics as described to show why free persons ought to be respected. I regard my second comment as decisive. The need for Rawls to settle on a sense of freedom that pins human dignity, in other words, the need for Rawls to settle on a comprehensive doctrine, will come back to haunt his other arguments.

Towards the end of *Political Liberalism*, Rawls again covers the grounding of the principles of justice in the original position. He again focuses on the basic rights and liberties, and especially the liberty of conscience. There are six arguments. Rawls organizes them around the moral powers of the human assumed to be in the original position. The first three arguments start from the second moral power—that is, the capacity for a concept of the good. In the first argument, Rawls assumes that in society the person has exercised this capacity and so is holding some concept of the good. But as placed in the original position, Rawls does not know what that concept of the good is. Rawls then says:

> [Representatives of the person] cannot take chances by permitting a lesser liberty of conscience to minority religions, say, on the possibility that those they represent espouse a majority or dominant religion and will therefore have an even greater liberty. For it may also happen that these persons belong to a minority faith and may suffer accordingly. If the parties were to gamble in this way, they would show that they did not take the religious, philosophical, or moral convictions of persons seriously, and, in effect, did not know what a religious, philosophical, or moral conviction was.[36]

In other words, since a world view is going to demand total commitment, but I do not know what view I hold, then I want the principles of justice in which freedom of conscience protects all world views.

Rawls' second and third arguments start from the capacity for some concept of the good as still unexercised. In the second argument, the capacity is looked upon as an extrinsic means to the realization of some concept of the good. The second argument is this:

> At any given moment this power serves the determinate conception of the good then affirmed; but the role of this power in forming other and more rational conceptions of the good and in revising existing ones must not be overlooked. There is no guarantee that all aspects of our present way of life are the most rational for us and not in need of at least minor if not major revision. For these reasons the adequate and full exercise of the capacity for a conception of the good is a means to a person's good. Thus, on the assumption that liberty of conscience, and therefore the liberty to fall into error and to make mistakes, is among the social conditions necessary for the development and

exercise of this power, the parties have another ground for adopting principles that guarantee this basic liberty.[37]

In sum, because the capacity for some concept of the good can be erroneous and so we can envisage ourselves over life going through a spectrum of world views, we would want to be safe in any of these cases. Liberty of conscience provides that safety.

The third argument is similar to the previous but adopts a slightly different starting point. The third argument begins from the capacity for a concept of the good, but now the capacity is regarded as part of our good. Rawls says,

> In this way of regarding the capacity for a conception of the good, this capacity is not a means to but is an essential part of a determinate conception of the good. The distinctive place in justice as fairness of this conception is that it enables us to view our final aims and loyalties in a way that realizes to the full extent one of the moral powers in terms of which persons are characterized in this political conception of justice. For this conception of the good to be possible, we must be allowed, even more plainly than in the case of the preceding ground, to fall into error and to make mistakes within the limits established by the basic liberties. In order to guarantee the possibility of this conception of the good, the parties, as our representatives, adopt principles which protect liberty of conscience.[38]

Here the moral need for self-perfection is more obviously seen to involve the realization of the capacity of the moral powers. Rawls describes this realization as coming to appreciate *why* our beliefs are true, and, as Mill would say, making our conception of the good "our own." All of which means that the concept of the good meets "the tests of our reason and . . . answer[s] to our deepest desires and affections."[39] In sum, the third argument claims that, since the moral capacity perfects us but can make mistakes, liberty of conscience should exist so that we are safe either way.

In his fourth, fifth, and sixth arguments, Rawls starts from the original position with the first moral power in mind—that is, from our capacity for a sense of justice. Rawls' fourth argument presumes that it is to everyone's good to have a just and stable scheme of cooperation. Rawls further describes such a scheme as "clear and perspicuous to our reason, congruent with and unconditionally concerned with our good, and rooted not in abnegation but in affirmation of our person."[40] Rawls then says this:

> That the two principles of justice are unconditionally concerned with everyone's good is shown by the equality of the basic liberties and their priority, as well as by the fair value of the political liberties (discussed in the next section) and the difference principle. For example, that the two principles of justice are unconditionally concerned with everyone's good is shown by the equality of the basic liberties and their priority, as well as by the fair value of the political liberties. Again, these principles are clear and perspicuous to our reason because they are to be public and mutually recognized, and they enjoin the basic liberties directly—on their face, as it were. These liberties do not depend upon conjectural calculations concerning the greatest net balance of social interests (or of social values). In justice as fairness such calculations have no place.[41]

In sum, because of the clarity and simplicity of the preceding arguments for the principles of justice, namely, that no utilitarian calculation is necessary to secure them, one can further argue that the principles express the criteria for the best scheme of justice, namely, one that is publicly knowable and congruent with our good.

The fifth argument begins from the original position with self-respect in mind. By Rawls' mention of self-respect, the reader might think that Rawls is at last ready to unveil the reasons for human dignity or the value in virtue of which a human commands respect and solicitude. I made much of this lacuna and the need to address it in my second comment to Rawls' argument for tolerance from the burdens of judgment. Actually, in argument five, Rawls is still *presuming* human dignity.

What the fifth argument does is to specify bases in the principles of justice that assure that everyone understands that they possess this dignity. In other words, self-respect means equality. Rawls says that the two principles of justice "are more effective than the other alternatives in encouraging and supporting self-respect of citizens as equal persons."[42] I see that I am the equal of you and am not a second-class citizen. Society is not a no-win situation for me. The contrary estimate kills self-respect with the tragic result that "nothing may seem worth doing and if some things have value for us, we lack a will to pursue them."[43] Hence, equality of citizenship is what I take Rawls to mean when he says that "self-respect is rooted in our self-confidence as a fully cooperating member of society capable of pursuing a worthwhile conception of the good over a complete life."[44]

Rawls strategizes that only the principles of justice provide the basic liberties that aid and abet self-respect. His fifth argument is this:

It is the content of these principles as public principles for the basic structure which has this result. This content has two aspects, each paired with one of the two elements of self-respect. Recall that the first element is our self-confidence as a fully cooperating member of society rooted in the development and exercise of the two moral powers . . .; the second element is our secure sense of our own value rooted in the conviction that we can carry out a worthwhile plan of life. The first element is supported by the basic liberties which guarantee the full and informed exercise of both moral powers. The second element is supported by the public nature of this guarantee and the affirmation of it by citizens generally, all in conjunction with the fair value of the political liberties and the difference principle. For our sense of our own value, as well as our self-confidence, depends on the respect and mutuality shown us by others.[45]

In sum, the basic liberties establish us as fully cooperating members of society because they, as mentioned, establish equality. Also, we can feel secure in this equality because of the public nature of the principles of justice, as mentioned in the fourth argument.

The sixth and last argument proceeds from the original position in light of a well-ordered society being a social union of social unions. To illustrate his meaning, Rawls mentions a group of musicians organized into an orchestra. In realizing a coordination of each musician's talents, the orchestra makes up for a deficiency in each musician alone. Importantly, Rawls also insists that the good of social union is most completely realized when everyone participates in this good. Hence, achieving the good of social unions requires a conception of persons as free and equal and, second, a notion of reciprocity. Without these requirements, the social good will be the work of others and so not participated in by all. Rawls concludes, "These attitudes are best secured by the two principles of justice precisely because of the recognized public purpose of giving justice to each citizen as a free and equal person on a basis of mutual respect."[46]

To begin comment on Rawls' six arguments, let me note that, like the argument from the burdens of judgment, all six contain a supposition. The assumption is that we ought to be respectful of our fellows especially in regard to the exercise of their moral powers. In short, we are owed a certain respect because we are free. From the perspective of his own comprehensive doctrine, a Thomist would agree. What Rawls calls the moral powers involves the intellection of being, and as an intellector of being, the human calls forth obligation. But Rawls simply leads us to freedom and leaves freedom unelaborated. How does this philosophically undeveloped notion of freedom generate respect in Rawls' mind?

The answer is embarrassingly simple. Because of the moral powers, humans create world views—philosophical, religious, and moral—about which humans can be quite fanatical. As Rawls said at the end of the first of his six arguments, if the parties in the original position gambled that their clients would be members of a majority religion, ". . . they would show that they did not take the religious, philosophical, or moral convictions of persons seriously, and, in effect, did not know what a religious, philosophical, or moral conviction was."[47]

What is, for example, religion? At the beginning of *Political Liberalism* and in contrast to ancient Greek civic religion, Rawls describes Catholicism as "authoritative, salvationist, and expansionist."[48] The effect of the Reformation was to proliferate this mindset among the Protestant sects. The further effect of the Reformation was religious wars. Tolerance and the acceptance of free faith emerged as the only alternative to endless war. The following is seminal for Rawls' work:

> What is new about this clash [between salvationist, creedal, and expansionist religions] is that it introduces into people's conceptions of their good a transcendent element not admitting of compromise. This element forces either mortal conflict moderated only by circumstance and exhaustion, or equal liberty of conscience and freedom of thought. Except on the basis of these last, firmly founded and publicly recognized, no reasonable political conception of justice is possible. Political liberalism starts by taking to heart the absolute depth of that irreconcilable latent conflict.[49]

Political liberalism is Rawls' position. Here Rawls acknowledges its starting point—irreconcilable religious conflict. So what is the answer to my query about Rawls' assumption of respect for humans? The answer is that respect is something that we afford each other because the alternative of not doing so is conflict. That is it; there is nothing deep here. And that is why political liberalism is freestanding. The stark alternatives of respect or war make it easy to understand why no references to a comprehensive doctrine are required for political liberalism.

Is this not a disappointment? Basically, respect for humans is like respect for a bomb. Respect is not a reaction to something positive but to a possible source of chaos. In other words, Rawls bases tolerance on power.

I should tolerate you because you can cause me trouble. But likewise, if you cannot cause me trouble, then I need not tolerate you. Tolerance is just for those in power. So again we are left simply hoping for tolerance. Among the vicissitudes of power, we just hope that those in power will respect those not in power. For all the high moral language of *Political Liberalism*, and some of it is very appealing to a Thomist, the political liberal is basically like a traffic cop hoping that no one will swerve a car into him.[50]

Rawls' inability to rationally integrate tolerance into political liberalism comes out strikingly in another way. Rawls acknowledges a social tendency in the principles of justice to eliminate religions. Any religious person would then balk at enlisting in the original position exercise. In discussing political liberalism's neutrality of aim, Rawls concedes that "it is surely impossible for the basic structure of a just constitutional regime not to have important effects and influences as to which comprehensive doctrines endure and gain adherents over time: and it is futile to try to counteract these effects and influences, or even to ascertain for political purposes how deep and pervasive they are. We must accept the facts of commonsense political sociology."[51]

For example, Rawls mentions that a child's education in a politically liberal society will include such things "as knowledge of their constitutional and civic rights so that, for example, they know that liberty of conscience exists in their society and that apostasy is not a legal crime."[52] Rawls admits a slippage, but concludes that "the unavoidable consequences of reasonable requirements for children's education may have to be accepted often with regret."[53] The best that Rawls can do is to insist that logically there is a great difference between comprehensive and political liberalism. But, to a religious person, the logical distinction is small consolation for the sociological dynamic. In fact, that dynamic would be a deal breaker. When in the original position, no person who might be religious in society would agree to Rawls' principles of justice. What religious person, especially with a family, would want to live in a society that works to undermine the religion? Hence, it is no surprise that radical orthodoxy proponents, like Tracey Rowland (whom I will discuss in chapter VI), argue that Catholics can no longer do business with Western liberalism and ought to retreat into a theocratic ghetto.

So, tolerance still seems to elude Rawls' grasp. In the parameters of Rawls' discussion, the correct conclusion, in my opinion, seems to be either a *modus vivendi* between the incommensurable worldviews of the ineradicable pluralism or, at worst, a return to religious wars. In other words, no advance on Rawls' initially mentioned first question and problem has been made.

How would one see it from the perspective of Aquinas' natural law ethics as described in this book? By Rawls' admission, political liberalism starts from the historical fact of the Reformation which he understands as presenting an unbridgeable pluralism. A Thomist would never concede that understanding and would see an error right there. One of the parties in this religiously divided group is not the juggernaut that Rawls depicts it to be. Rather, it possesses the resources to be a leader in tolerance. That group is Catholicism.

The bases for my claim are many. In this book, my basis is the Church's spokesman of theology, Thomas Aquinas. As I explained in chapter I, Aquinas understands theology in such a way that the theologian cannot but also philosophize. I have been calling attention to one point of his philosophizing—namely, Aquinas' philosophical understanding of human psychology. Because of that psychology, Aquinas would never admit unbridgeable comprehensive doctrines. Functioning in the minds of all is the one psychology of the intellection of being more or less understood.

As I concluded at the end of chapter III, the intellection of being is the central theme about the human. Fundamentally and always, even if we do not realize it, we face each other as fellow intellectors of being; that is the stage upon which human existence is played. In chapter VI, I will try to make this conclusion more concrete by dovetailing it into Christopher Dawson's narrative of cultural history. Importantly, Dawson's narrative treats the Reformation.

What I am claiming is that Rawls' account of democracy is one account. And in the reflection of people of goodwill, it should not be anointed. Rawls' account fails to secure the tolerance that it seeks. Another account of democracy builds upon the Thomistic thesis of a common psychology. Hence, a religious person need not see democracy as a trap. A dear one's move to another comprehensive doctrine will not appear as an ineradicable loss. There always remains the appeal to dialogue from the resources of natural reason.

This thesis of the intellection of being keeps the Thomist in the dialogical position that I outlined in chapter IV. Likewise, no non-Thomist should balk at my Thomist account of democracy because of fear of emerging from the original position into a Thomistic society. My Thomistic interpretation can also underwrite, like no one else, Rawls' two principles. The freedom of conscience that is the basic liberty in the first principle is echoed by the understanding of the human as an intellector of being. Intellect must address intellect. This demand is strictly entailed and is not something for which we must simply hope.

The chances of contact between the parties are greatly increased because Aquinas' psychology is more than his logic. As I explained in chapter II, Aquinas' psychology enables the Thomist to understand how the intellection of being can be unappreciated, or only dimly so, and result in disagreements about the precepts of his natural law ethics. Sources of occlusion are the passions, sensible things themselves as the sources of our abstractive knowledge of being, and the direct realist focus of human cognition. But the feints and twists of the *ratio entis* in the human mind are still more varied than these three.

As I will explain when I discuss Rorty, shortly (and Dawson, much later), the notion of being can become merely associated with things, especially the spatially or temporally great and small, so that faux epiphanies of being are created. Such confusion can invest things with a preciousness that they do not in truth have. Nevertheless, as an automatic and spontaneous abstraction, the notion of being is present in the minds of all, and it produces certain effects. The clever Thomist can admit and acknowledge these effects in the lives of others and patiently lead them to appreciate the larger truth. The Thomist's understanding of these twists and turns of the mind creates a better opportunity for open dialogue than hitting one's opponent only with a strict syllogism.

For example, if Rawls is the interlocutor, then, as a Thomist, I would direct my efforts to Rawls' following admissions. In Rawls' argument for tolerance from the burdens of judgment, a major premise is that equal should be compared with equal. Because a denial of this premise implies that being and nonbeing are not different, then the premise implies the noncontradiction principle. So, being is present and Rawls should be open to hearing what a Thomist has to say. Rawls' admissions of freedom can also be massaged to bring out the presence of being in the human mind with the consequent development of human dignity. Finally, Rawls' talk of "conceptions of the good" implies a commonality in all these conceptions. This insight should open the interlocutor to Aquinas' discussions of the richness of analogical concepts and especially to the richness of being whose acknowledged presence in our minds transforms our understanding of human relations.

Rawls' second principle of justice insists upon a debt that those better-off in society owe to those less well-off. Rawls also calls it the difference principle. His reasoning for the second principle as it applies to private property is as follows:

> The two principles also specify an ideal form for the basic structure in the light of which ongoing institutional procedural processes are constrained and adjusted. Among these constraints are the limits on the accumulation of property (especially if private property in productive assets exists) that derive from the requirements of the fair value of political liberty and fair equality of opportunity, and the limits based on considerations of stability and excusable envy, both of which are connected to the essential primary good of self-respect. We need such an ideal to guide the adjustments necessary to preserve background justice. As we have seen, even if everyone acts fairly as defined by the rules that they are both reasonable and practicable to impose on individuals, the upshot of many separate transactions will eventually undermine background justice.[54]

In light of the initial sentence, I read this passage in the context of the previous analysis of Rawls on tolerance. Hence, the social parties are the parties of the original position—that is, the parties that have the power to cause trouble. So the parties for which society must be frequently adjusted are the parties that can cause trouble because they have power. If you are powerless, then you *may* get some adjustment in your behalf. But that solicitude is contingent with the logic of power. If you are an intellector of being, however, then you *should* get some adjustment in your behalf. So, what I call fraternal tolerance seems to be echoed in Rawls' difference principle, but it is far from secured by his freestanding political liberalism, as I understand it. Finally, as I explained in preceding sections of this chapter, the same difficulty of logically integrating fraternal tolerance is found in hedonism, utilitarianism, and Kantianism. Only if you have the power to cause trouble will you get concessions from these philosophies.

In sum, a person in the original position should not fear ending up a postmodern, for example, in a Thomistic society. As I will note in my next section, like Rawls, the postmodernist on postmodern terms can only hope for tolerance. In chapter IV, I pointed out that the Thomistic mindset obliges the Thomist to listen to and to converse with fellow humans. Hence, in the section on Heidegger, I noted that the Thomist hears and understands the postmodern love of creativity and the anguish to which the love of creativity can lead. The Thomist tries to address both by tracing the inspiration to creativity to the intellection of being. Art attempts to mimic the release of analogates from being. The artist is not unfaithful to that inspiration through fidelity to spouse or to fellows. The artist can see that the source of the artist's inspiration is most intensely present in them.

But speaking more practically, will not a postmodernist, who is, for example, a pragmatist, want to address social problems in ways different from a Thomist? The pragmatist sees the solution to the problem of over-population to lie in contraception and abortion. Will not those approaches mean that a pragmatist would never opt to live in a Thomist society? They should not. In elaborating the thought of the prophet of pragmatism, Francis Bacon, John Dewey took pains to explain that in pragmatism scientific power was now, not for the Empire of Man over Man, but for the Empire of Man over Nature.[55] This admission that the power of science ought to be aimed at nature and not at man expresses a common ground from which discussion of social problems can profitably begin.

4. Rorty and Tolerance through Sympathy

A defender of Rawls and of contemporary American democracy is Richard Rorty.[56] Rorty is aware of the power dynamic in Rawls' political liberalism and of the challenges the dynamic creates for tolerance. In an article on ethnocentrism, Rorty acknowledges the past treatment and present plight of the Indians in American democracy: "The vast majority of nineteenth-century Americans took no more notice of them than they did of criminal psychopaths or village idiots. The Indians, whether drunk or sober, were non-persons, without human dignity, means to our grandparents' ends."[57] But Rorty explains that our attitudes have changed as a result of one of the two groups serving the moral tasks of liberal democracy—the agents of love. These agents are "specialists in particularity." Rorty identifies them with historians, novelists, ethnographers, and muckraking journalists. These specialists gradually expand the imagination of those in power so that the term *we* includes more different sorts of people.[58]

In a 1994 essay, "Feminism and Pragmatism," Rorty connects this expansion of imagination to Rawls' original position. By expanding the imagination, specialists of particularity produce new sorts of "concrete others" whom one might turn out to be.[59] But Rorty's contribution to Rawls still seems opaque. For example, how does an expansion of the powerful white man's imagination lead to greater love of the Indian? If parties with the power to cause trouble carve out Rawls' principles of justice, then why would the Indians be included in a discussion about appropriate principles of justice? Why would a white man ever worry about turning out to be an Indian? Do the particularity specialists somehow empower the powerless? Not quite. Rorty has added a new factor to Rawls.

A year earlier in "Human Rights, Rationality, and Sentimentality," Rorty described this new factor. From the context of his pragmatism, Rorty claims that "the human rights culture seems to owe nothing to increased moral knowledge, and everything to hearing sad and sentimental stories."[60] What do the sad stories do? Appealing to Hume, Rorty answers that the stories appeal to our fundamental moral capacity—sympathy. Moral progress consists in a progress of sentiments. Rorty elaborates, "This progress consists in an increasing ability to see the similarities between ourselves and people very unlike us as outweighing the differences. It is the result of what I have been calling 'sentimental education.' The relevant similarities are not a matter of sharing a deep true self that instantiates true humanity, but are such little, superficial similarities as cherishing our parents and our children—similarities that do not distinguish us in any interesting way from nonhuman animals."[61]

Also, "By 'sympathy' I mean the sort of reactions Athenians had more of after seeing Aeschylus's *The Persians* than before, the sort that whites in the United States had more of after reading *Uncle Tom's Cabin* than before, the sort we have more of after watching television programs about the genocide in Bosnia."[62]

For Rorty, the powerful are not so powerful that they are also unsympathetic. The capacity to feel sympathy should be added to Rawls' description of them. By their sad and sentimental stories, the specialists in particularity, the agents of love, are also the agents of tolerance in a democratic society: "Such stories, repeated and varied over the centuries, have induced us, the rich, safe, powerful people, to tolerate and even to cherish powerless people."[63]

With Rorty's reference to Hume, and so supposedly to a comprehensive philosophical doctrine, a reader might well wonder if Rawls would admit this emendation to his political liberalism. Not doing so, however, still leaves Rawls with the problem of accommodating tolerance. But granting the emendation, does it do the job? Only sometimes, and that contingency is what Rorty admits is a prima facie problem for his inclusion of tolerance through sympathy.

In the above mentioned "Human Rights" article, Rorty continues, "I think this persistence [for something stronger than sentiment] is due mainly to a semiconscious realization that if we hand our hopes for moral progress over to sentiment, we are in effect handing them over to *condescension.* For we shall be relying on those who have the power to change things—people like the rich New England abolitionists or rich bleeding hearts like Robert Owen and Friedrich Engels—rather than relying on something that has power over them."[64] The specter of condescension expresses my recurrent problem with all of the positions that I discuss in this chapter. My problem is that the positions do not logically entail tolerance. At best, they logically entail only the hope for tolerance.

Rorty is quite aware of the desire for a knockdown reason for tolerance, but he insists, à la Nietzsche, that the desire is driven by resentment.[65] The powerful are so hurtful that we desire to hurt them back. The fulfillment of that desire consists in creating guilt in the powerful because they have violated some "reason" for tolerance. Of course, for Rorty, no knockdown reason exists.[66] Hence, Rorty insists that we should all get over our resentment and accept the contingency of tolerance, not as a problem or an objection, but as the best hope that we have.

I want to insist that the contingency of tolerance thesis remains a problem for Rorty. I begin by admitting that there is some plausibility to Rorty's claim that resentment is the basis of dissatisfaction with the thesis. For if they are clever enough, the agents of love—journalists, anthropologists, historians, novelists, and the like—can evoke sympathy for anything. In their professional activities seems to exist a wildness that makes one wonder about the accuracy of what they are describing. Hence, the powerful can just shake off the magic and insist that particularity is only particularity. For example, displays of baby Hitler pictures and descriptions of his youth begin to create a sympathy for Hitler that is inappropriately freaky for the Nazi leader. Likewise inappropriate is the sympathy created for the ancient Chinese sites inundated by the Three Gouges Dam—and for snail darters. Hence, the powerful conclude, for example, that the sympathy created for near-extinct cultures of the Northwest Indian tribes is no big deal. They conclude further that it is out of resentment alone that purveyors of particularity create the illusion that something precious is present, something that commands our respect. But particularity is only particularity. The powerful may go for the story or they may not. Hence, we have the contingency of tolerance.

But the source of the illusion, of the magic, still requires an explanation. After all, if particularity is just particularity, from whence the magic? Rorty's reference to Hume on sympathy will not do. Hume explains sympathy in terms of passions, or vivid ideas, stirred up (*pace* Hume's objections to knowing causality) by the perception of the causes or effects of passions in others. As an example, Hume describes one observing the preparations for an operation in Hume's time. These observations cause passions of terror in us that evoke our sympathy for the patient. [67] But with a reader of the writings of the specialists of particularity—Harriet Beecher Stowe's for example—where are the passions to evoke the sympathies? The magic can occur in the quiet and solitude of a reading room. For those occasions of sympathy, what is the explanation?

Sympathy seems to be a topic in need of further elucidation. Rorty's position seems vulnerable to out-narration. I see Aquinas' psychology of the intellection of being as providing what is needed. This psychology also goes a long way toward explaining the persistence of the contingency objection. In my second chapter, I explained how Aquinas could understand ethical relativism. Because of his abstractive epistemology, Aquinas can understand things as hiding being while they reveal being. Hence, the notion of being can be implicit in the minds of all and causing effects on the conscious level. Among these effects is a sense of human dignity even in proponents of recreational sex and euthanasia. But once abstracted, being can also play a second trick. The notion of being, the *ratio entis*, can create faux epiphanies of being. In these cases, being does not have the intensity of presence found in intellectors of being. Because of certain superficial characteristics of things, being can become simply associated with things. This association suffices to invest the things with the implications of being itself.

As I noted in chapter I, one of these implications is being as the good. Since, unlike a univocal intelligible object, being does not abstract from the differences of its instances, the mind apprehends being as an intelligible concrescence of perfection. As such, being is the desirable par excellence and, so, is denominated the good. So, for example, the contemplation of the gargantuan can unwittingly enlist the aid of being—up and against which the gargantuan can be profiled and so objectified. Hence, the gargantuan can take on all the preciousness of being itself. That is why, to an American Indian on the western plains, the mountain is something mystical. The Indian unknowingly mixes the experience of the mountain with his intellection of being. The scientist's insistence that the mountain is just a basalt dome is so focused with minutiae that the association of the mountain with being is lost. Yet if the scientist is not careful, being can break though in the scientist's consideration of minutiae. For in order to contemplate the small, everything else must be gotten rid of. The result is that the small stands alone with being. Because of that cognitive association, the small can become invested with the preciousness of being itself. Hence, the reverential and awe-filled remark of that popularizer of current science, Carl Sagan, that we are all "star stuff."

Not only spatial minutiae but temporal minutiae can suffer the same association with being. Consider the experience of viewing old photographs. Even if the subjects bear no relation to the viewer and even if the subjects are ordinary, at certain moments, the pictures can take on a poignancy. Out of all possible moments, we, the viewers, are at *that* moment. Just as the contemplation of physical minutiae enlists the aid of being, so too does the contemplation of temporal minutiae. Moreover, because we know that we are looking at a moment in the past, the poignancy includes a note of sadness. Why? By its association with what is past, being is experienced as suffering an eclipse.

This psychology of an association with the *abstractum* of being is, in my opinion, the explanation of an experience related to me by a grade-school friend. The friend would contemplate himself standing at the opposite side of the schoolyard and then enjoy making it real by walking to that side. What was the fun in this apparently trite exercise? I think that the exercise drew its joy from the fact that out of all possibilities, my friend was picking out that one. In his mind, the picking out left the possibility alone with being and thus allowed it to draw some of the preciousness of being. Making the possibility actual was then appreciated as making something very precious actual—hence, his joy.

Yet, in these cases, it must be insisted that the relation to being is not quite accurate. Certain features of the data inappropriately aggrandize the relation of the data to being. If one does not realize what is going on, the data can take on all the value of being itself. Again, consider the spontaneous reaction of adults to a young child or baby. Both the child and the baby are "so precious." Just as the consideration of minutiae entails a vacating from consciousness of everything else, so that the minutiae stand alone with being, so too does the consideration of the fragility and helplessness of the child and baby. Their perceived vulnerability is a reaction to their isolation. Unlike an adult, they have not yet effected relations that establish them in existence. But even though, as yet, they are isolated from everything else, they are not in our awareness isolated from being. In fact, the association with being is intensified as their dissociation from other things is increased. Here the experience of the children as precious has everything to do with their association to being.

The above analysis illustrates that some of the most striking perceptions of human dignity do not always derive from the correct source. The unwitting psychic association of the child or infant up and against being seems sufficient to generate, in everyday experience, a modicum of respect for these small humans. In fact, it is a more persistent source of human dignity than Kantian reflections on the autonomy of the will, Aquinas' understanding of the person as an intellector of being, and even Christian revelation on the direct relation of the person to God. Nevertheless, the "wildness" of this psychology, —that is, in its applicability to anything—belies it as truly locating the basis of human dignity. That true philosophical source of dignity for all humans, Thomistically speaking, is the intimate relation of the rational soul to the *ratio entis*.

The point that I wish to make is that knowing the correct relation of being to a thing is crucial for understanding sentimental reactions. Is the thing a true epiphany of being as is the human intellector, the creator, spousal union, and society (and still distinctions are necessary here), or is the thing merely cognitively associated with being? In other words, with an epiphany of being, the nature of the thing involves being. There is an intrinsic intensity of the *ratio entis*. On the other hand, the thing's relation to being can be more superficial. Certain accidents, such as physical or temporal size, can prompt a use of being in our awareness of the thing. The merely associative play of being always invests things with a worth out of all proportion to the truth. Hence, Aquinas argues that happiness is not to be found in the motions of the will. Joy and delight are not to be trusted. Aquinas explains, "Now, in their relation to the will act, true happiness does not differ from false happiness. In fact, the will, when it desires, loves, or enjoys, is related in just the same way to its object, whatever it may be that is presented to it as a highest good, whether truly or falsely. Of course, whether the object so presented is truly the highest good, or is false, this distinction is made on the part of the intellect."[68] The intellect's discerning work consists in differentiating an epiphany of being from a mere, albeit intense, association with being.

Without realizing it, Rorty's specialists of particularity are deeply involved with the associative play of being. Their descriptive emphasis on particularity indicates that the associative play of being is either with physical or temporal minutiae. Such descriptions isolate the subject from other things and so, in that way, associate the subject with being and prompt an endearment of the subject. But because the matter is simply one of association, only a faux epiphany of being results. Hence, there is no guarantee of a sympathetic reaction in others.

Rorty is quite right to insist on the contingency of tolerance. As the scientist said to the Indian, "The mountain is just a mountain," so the powerful can say to the agents of tolerance that a tyrant is just a tyrant, an ethnic cleansing is just an ethnic cleansing. The powerful can insist that they do not see the value in the fact. Yet, this same psychology for faux epiphanies also reveals why proponents of particularity will never be satisfied by the contingency of tolerance, as Rorty insists they should.

According to Aquinas' philosophical psychology, there cannot be a faux epiphany of being without a true epiphany of being. Only if it is intellected can being be merely associated with something—the gargantuan or the minute. So the idea, dim as it may be, that something is owed tolerance will be ineradicable. To insist on tolerance is to be acting not out of resentment but out of an inchoate awareness of oneself as an intellector of being. Rorty's intuition of the poignancy of concrete writing has a depth that his pragmatism, with its anti-metaphysical and anti-realist views, does not allow him to investigate. Hence, Rorty can only present us with the hope for tolerance. It is unclear that Rorty achieves much of an advance on the problems in Rawls.

5. Legislation

In sum, the common good and its constitutive factors are something that any philosophy must accommodate. The same test that has been imposed upon Aquinas' natural law ethics must also be applied to the philosophies that criticize natural law. My claim is that these philosophies, not Thomism, fail the test. And just as Thomism acquired a pariah status because of its perceived antipathy to tolerance, so too, and more deservedly so, should these philosophies. The ticket into public discussion is a philosophy's logical embrace of the common good. Only such a philosophy, logically embracing the commmon good, can be a genuine philosophy of democratic government. Needless to say, a society has the right to apply the same test to religions as well as to philosophies.

Again, I have been speaking of how a society would defend the tolerance component of the common good without prohibiting philosophies or religions that do not logically accommodate it. I have already mentioned the attitude of the Thomist, actually the attitude of any authentic philosopher, to counter idea with idea, to have diamond cut diamond, and not to appeal to extra-philosophical means to settle philosophical disputes. Hence, no Thomist would want to see opponents outlawed. The responsibility of the state is not to settle philosophical arguments but to protect the common good through its legislation. So the state can act in regard to the above mentioned philosophies only when their most threatening practical implications come to bear on the common good. Hence, no neo-Nazi will ever get to carry out his theory of racial supremacy, and if he tried, then his attack on the common good would be met by the protectors of society's laws. Somewhat similarly in the United States, desegregation laws were federally enforced.

Also, sexual hedonists who promote a simply recreational use of sexuality attack the common good by denying society's future members. Unless a society intends to commit suicide, it should never concede the premise of the sexual hedonist that sexual activity is whatever you want it to be. So, how do legislators deal with sexual hedonists? In this day, sexual hedonism has become an industry. As a result, sexual hedonism has acquired vast sums of money that have allowed it to take on a life of its own. If unregulated, the merchandizing of sex simply for individual satisfaction would ruin society. So my suggestion is that legislators should regulate the sex industry, just as it regulates other industries, such as the tobacco and fast-food industries. Hence, legislators can pass laws that regulate the advertisement and display of a hedonistic lifestyle and that hamper the distribution of pornography to the young. The state could also extensively tax the sale of pornographic material. To avoid inciting violence and causing health issues, the state can prohibit live sex shows at "adult" establishments. Furthermore, to avoid giving the impression to the young that by these regulations the state is somehow sanctioning these activities among adults, pornographic material can be required to prominently display the warning "promiscuity is hazardous to your health" as cigarette packages similarly warn about tobacco use. Admonitions to use condoms is not enough. Again, with cigarettes, the state does not advise people to smoke filter cigarettes; the state advises people not to smoke at all.

Hopefully these will be laws that not only protect the common good from behaviors that attack it, but they will also be laws that send a message to certain people to rethink their lifestyles. Somewhat similarly, desegregation laws not only prohibit the practice of segregation. They also send a message to segregationists that members of the society ought to have other values. In sum, legislation here could mimic legislation that harasses smokers. Though society permits smoking, society also passes legislation that makes smoking difficult and expensive to practice. Why should not the same be done with the sex industry?

How far laws regulating sexual hedonism, bigotry, smoking (and such) should go is a prudential judgment. The U.S. government acted decisively in the case of desegregation. In America, the line is drawn at public sex and prostitution. You can see a striptease, view photos, and read erotic books. But you cannot legally spend money to view live sex or to get it. Even the vices allowed by law vary in emphasis in different states. Whether my country has correctly drawn the line only time will tell. As I mentioned, the sex industry is now so big that it has a life of its own. One can wonder if any of these regulations have any effect. Consider the minimal effects of regulation on the tobacco industry. This point has led others to say that more drastic measures are needed.

But it is also worth noting that, besides restricting civil law to the protection of the common good, Aquinas also insisted in the *Summa Theologiae* I-II, 96, 2c, that, under pain of causing a disrespect of the law among the members of society, law should be proportioned to what the moral character of the people can bear. Just as an overbearing parent can crush the spirit of the child, so too overbearing laws can crush the spirit of the citizenry. So perhaps the wisest public course is to continue with regulations that socially ostracize patrons of the sex industry and to hope that spontaneous movements among the citizenry can deal with the challenge. Regarding the use of alcohol, U.S. constitutional prohibition backfired while the temperance movements in Eastern Europe succeeded.

6. Heretics

I want to discuss two counterclaims to my recommendation of Aquinas. In sum, given what Aquinas says about treatment of heretics and Jews, Aquinas cannot be the proponent of tolerance that I have described. This treatment of heretics and Jews is described by Aquinas in the articles of questions 10 and 11 in the second half of the second part of his *Summa Theologiae*. On its face, Aquinas' position on the treatment of heretics, described in article 3 of question 11, sounds very intolerant. Aquinas says that heretics should be given two offers to repent. If they do not repent, they should be excommunicated and handed over to the civil government for execution. Aquinas allows toleration of heretics only if the Church's prosecution would be so indiscriminate that the prosecution threatens the innocent.

Aquinas' stand against heretics certainly seems to be incompatible with my presentation on Thomism and tolerance. As I repeated above, intellectual disagreements must be solved intellectually; diamond must cut diamond. Also, except in extreme cases, the state has no role here. So, has my presentation got Aquinas wrong? I do not think so. Aquinas' position on heretics appears intolerant because the contemporary reader assumes that the heretic has a genuine intellectual disagreement with Catholicism and is just following his conscience. But that is not the individual about whom Aquinas writes.

For Aquinas, the heretic is guilty of the sin of unbelief.[69] But sin is a type of human act.[70] And since, properly speaking, a human act is a voluntary act— an act of will performed with knowledge[71]—then to be a sinner one must knowingly and willingly do evil. Hence, the heretic is a person who knows that Catholicism is true but freely decides to oppose Catholic truth and to take others with him.[72] In short, Aquinas' understanding of the heretic is analogous to society's understanding of a citizen who commits treason, that is, someone who betrays his country to another country for a sum of money.

According to Aquinas' understanding, the heretic is attacking the spiritual common good just as much as someone who commits treason is attacking the temporal common good. Hence, just as no one could criticize the state for defending itself against treasonous citizens, so too, no one should criticize the Church for defending itself against heretics. Also, though unmentioned by Aquinas, I would like to note that, in Aquinas' time, the Catholic Church was the cradle of civil society. Though the temporal and spiritual spheres were theoretically distinguished, civil society had not reached its maturity and rightful autonomy. Because of this historical state of affairs, the heretic's attack upon the Church was, de facto, also an attack upon society. Hence, subsequent to the judgment of the Church, the heretic could not only be excommunicated by the Church but could also be executed by the civil authorities. In our present day, civil society has reached maturity, and so the Church restricts its dealings with heretics to excommunication and the battle of ideas. As mentioned above, civil authorities would become involved only when the practical results of a religion seriously threaten the temporal common good.

Aquinas is well aware that, though the logical implications of the category of heretic are clear, applying the category to particular persons is often far from clear. In that latter respect, rash judgments can be made and the innocent can be swept up with the guilty. Accordingly, Aquinas insists that the authorities ought to suffer the cockles with the wheat until it becomes perfectly plain to everyone involved that the individual with whom one is dealing is a heretic in Aquinas' sense.[73] I am sure that some will insist that such a point of clear knowledge is never reached. But others will disagree. Consider Neville Chamberlain's realization that he had been lied to by Hitler. Sometimes it is perfectly obvious who our sworn enemies are.

7. Jews

One must maintain this same perspective when one is reading Aquinas on the treatment of the Jews. In short, as discussed by Aquinas, both the heretic and the Jew are sinners. Both are guilty of the sin of unbelief. Hence, Aquinas is considering both to have voluntarily turned their backs to the truth of Christ. The only difference is that the heretic sins after having accepted Christ, while the Jewish unbeliever rejects Christ without having accepted Christ.[74] Again, Aquinas' approach to both heretics and Jews in terms of the category of the sin of unbelief means that Aquinas is not speaking of all Jews.

Many Jews, if not most, rise just to the level of the religion of their parents and never go on to explicitly reject Christianity with an understanding of its correctness. Aquinas is not speaking about these Jews. He is dealing with a category of what he considers the possible—a human who knows that Christ is the Messiah but who freely rejects this truth and intends its destruction. Aquinas thought that instances of this type existed. That is a factual judgment, and it is a factual judgment that must be made with all the reserve mentioned above. Whether Aquinas was correct in making it, I leave to the discernment of historians. As a philosopher, my concern is only with the correctness of Aquinas' logical implications from the category.

This narrow focus is important to address the criticisms of John Y. B. Hood in his *Aquinas and the Jews*.[75] Although Hood acknowledges that, on Jewish issues, "Aquinas adopted a relatively tolerant position,"[76] Hood maintains that Aquinas' theological positions logically imply a much more intolerant position. According to Hood, Aquinas is not bothered by the logical inconsistency because Aquinas' intention is only to justify actual Church practice towards the Jews.[77] Hood argues his thesis by criticizing Aquinas' determinations of four topics: the distinction between heretics and Jews, the baptizing of the children of Jews, the right of Jews to worship, and norms for relations with unbelievers. I want to critique Hood's analyses of these topics. In particular, I want to illustrate that Hood's claim of intolerance follows only if one assumes another meaning of *Jew* than the one described above.

First, Hood argues that Aquinas' distinction between heretics and Jews is weakly drawn, and so, logically, Jews should be treated like heretics. I have described the treatment of heretics. Heretics should be forced to repent under pain of death. Hence, Aquinas' treatment of Jews is intolerant. Hood provides two reasons for the weakness of the distinction. First, given Aquinas' idea of the prefigurative function of the Jewish Law, "even ordinary Jews had professed an implicit belief in [Christ] each time they obeyed one of the Law's ceremonial precepts."[78] Hence, ordinary Jews, like heretics, were in effect rejecting the truth of Christ.

Hood himself acknowledges a weakness in this first reason. He says, "A great deal rides on this distinction between accepting a symbol of the faith and acknowledging its reality." In truth, the weakness lies elsewhere. To be a heretic is to be a sinner, and to sin one must willingly do what one knows to be evil. Hence, to be a heretic one must reject an explicit belief in Christ. Again, the heretic is not like a conscientious objector who has an honest intellectual confusion. The heretic is more like a betrayer of one's country who knows that his country is good and that he should remain patriotic but for love of money betrays his country. So, even granting that ordinary Jews by their practices profess an implicit belief in Christ, this fact does not make them heretics. Importantly, Hood's first reason does reveal an assumption in his reading of Aquinas—namely, that in Aquinas' texts, *Jew* means an ordinary Jew.[79]

Hood's second reason does acknowledge that in Aquinas' discussions *Jews* sometimes means unbelievers in the sense of sinners. Hood notes that, for Aquinas, "both the Pharisees and priests knew Jesus was the Messiah."[80] Hence, should not these Jews receive the same treatment as heretics, and so is not Aquinas' treatment at least of these Jews intolerant? I do not think so. I have explained above that Aquinas' treatment of heretics is not intolerant. So even granting Hood's claim of equivalency, Hood's conclusion does not follow. Remember, if *Jew* is equivalent to *heretic*, then Aquinas is not speaking of all Jews but only those Jews who know the truth of Christ and seek to destroy it. But is there a logical equivalency? Aquinas does not think so. As I noted, heretics not only know the truth of Christ, they also professed it. Jewish unbelievers never professed this truth that they reject. Hence, the Church for her common spiritual good can exercise compulsion over heretics without any violation of the conscience of the heretic.[81]

With other unbelievers one can exercise compulsion only to defend Christians from the aggression of unbelievers: "It is for this reason that

Christ's faithful often wage war with unbelievers, not indeed for the purpose of forcing them to believe, because even if they were to conquer them, and take them prisoners, they should still leave them free to believe, if they will, but in order to prevent them from hindering the faith of Christ."[82] Aquinas' given reason is that "to believe depends on the will." Where is the intolerance in Aquinas' position? Do not Christians have a right to defend themselves? Again, the specter of intolerance rears itself only if one assumes that *Jew* means the ordinary Jew. In sum, Hood provides no reasons for ordinary Jews to worry about some extrapolation to them of Aquinas' treatment of heretics.

Secondly, Hood investigates the topic of Aquinas on the baptizing of Jewish children. At *Summa Theologiae* II–II, 10, 12, Aquinas gives two arguments against such a practice. Though Aquinas' determination of the question sounds quite tolerant, Hood focuses upon the second argument to bring out a wickedness in Aquinas' resolution. Using natural law, Aquinas says that before reaching the age of reason, the child naturally belongs to its parents. And so, baptizing a child of Jewish parents would be a violation of natural justice. For Hood, Aquinas' position is wicked because Aquinas uses it against the second objection listed in the article. The second objection states, "One is more bound to succor a man who is in danger of everlasting death, than one who is in danger of temporal death. Now it would be a sin, if one saw a man in danger of temporal death and failed to go to his aid. Since, then, the children of Jews and other unbelievers are in danger of everlasting death, should they be left to their parents who would imbue them with their unbelief, it seems that they ought to be taken away from them and baptized, and instructed in the faith."[83]

Hood's comment is this: "Aquinas was in all sincerity advocating that children be allowed to burn in hell rather than permit society to violate the rights of parents. If we moderns took hell as seriously as we take child abuse, his attitude would appear monstrous."[84] But Hood misreads the objection. It is not the child as a child that is in danger of eternal death but the child as an adult imbued with the unbelief of his parents. Again, it is the sinner who is damned and the sinner is one who willingly does what he knows to be evil. No child as a child—before the age of reason—could be a sinner and so no child as a child goes to hell, as Hood is claiming.[85] Hood is knocking down a straw man of his own making.

Third, Hood looks at the thoughts of Aquinas, at *Summa Theologiae* II-II, 10, 11, on the rights of Jews to worship. Aquinas argues that Jewish rites should be tolerated because they give symbolic witness to Christian truth.[86] The rites of other unbelievers, which are neither truthful nor profitable, are not to be tolerated, except to avoid a greater evil. Hood finds Aquinas' position on Jewish rites ridiculous. First, he says, "For symbols to be meaningful, however, someone must understand them. Aquinas solves this problem adroitly. Once the *sapientes* among the Jews understood the prophetic significance of the Mosaic rituals, but now it is Christians—the new *sapientes*—who understand their true meaning. But symbols must also be perceived if they are to signify, and Thomas does not make it clear just how Christians were supposed to observe Jews performing the symbolic rituals of the Law."[87]

For secondly, "Canon law forbade [Christians] from attending a circumcision rite, observing Passover, or even sharing a meal with Jews, and certainly Thomas did not call for the repeal of such prohibitions. To be sure, Christians could study the Pentateuch. . . . But they did not need actual Jews in their midst to do this."[88] Hence, the Church's own segregationist policies subvert Aquinas' rationale for tolerating Jewish worship.

Hood observes (on page 93) that Aquinas could have argued his position by appeal to the inviolability of the will or the duty to follow the dictates of conscience. But then his argument would allow pagans, and perhaps heretics, to worship God as they saw fit, and so the argument would prove too much. I would add to the speculation by observing that another implication of Hood's criticism is that Jewish worship would be insufficiently distinguished from pagan worship, and so Jewish worship would suffer the same lack of tolerance as pagan worship.

I agree that, to be meaningful, symbols must be understandable by someone. But with Hood I wonder about the victory if only Christians, even the *sapientes*, understand the symbolic meaning of the Jewish rites. But furthermore, if the Jews about whom Aquinas is speaking are ordinary Jews, who like ordinary Christians, believe that their religion is the right one, then does not Aquinas' claim of enemies bearing witness to the Christian faith ring hollow? Hence, I think that we must remember that the Jews about whom Aquinas is speaking are unbelievers in the formal sense—that is, Jews who know that Christ is the Messiah but reject Christ nevertheless. As far as I can tell, Hood never reads the texts with this category in mind. And if the category were brought to his attention, he would probably resent it. Nevertheless, Aquinas thinks that the category is possible. Moreover, Aquinas thinks that the category has been instantiated, though, as mentioned, I leave that judgment of fact to historians.

Hence, for Aquinas, the symbolic value of the Jewish rites are understood by two parties—Jewish unbelievers and Christians. The victory over Aquinas' enemies consists in the thought that people who reject Christ knowingly perform acts that in fact proclaim Christ. Such behavior is as frustrating as being forced to publicly honor the accomplishments of a colleague whom one hates because of jealousy. Lastly, it is unclear why the Church's "segregationist policies" undermine this understanding of Aquinas' argument. To appreciate the symbol, Christians need not attend Jewish rituals but simply know that unbelievers practice them. Likewise, the above mentioned colleague, although absent from the ceremony, derives some satisfaction just from knowing that his enemies publicly honor him.

Finally, Hood looks at Aquinas' treatment (at *Summa Theologiae* II-II, 10) of relations with Jews. At article 9, Aquinas restricts legitimate Jewish/Christian contact to two types: contact that may lead to conversion of Jews and contact arising from economic needs of Christians. Hood describes Aquinas' position as "essentially manipulative."[89] At article 10, Aquinas argues that Jews should not have "dominion" over Christians because subordinates are inclined to adopt the views of their superiors. Nor should unbelievers hold an office of authority over Christian since, if they knew the faults of Christians, unbelievers would come to despise the faith: "Et similiter infideles contemnunt fidem si fidelium defectus cognoscant." Lastly, Hood notes (on pages 97 and 98) that, in disputations with unbelievers, Aquinas says (in article 7) that the disputation is not to be conducted as if matters of faith were in doubt.[90] Hood interprets this to mean that Christians would completely control the debate and place restraints upon unbelievers.

In my opinion , Hood's claim that Christian contact with Jews is "essentially manipulative" makes sense if one is thinking of ordinary Jews. Such Jews are simply following their consciences. With them in mind, Aquinas' restrictions seem to lack the honesty found between all people of goodwill. But again, the Jews about whom Aquinas is speaking are those guilty of the sin of unbelief. Hence, Aquinas is speaking about those who are willingly doing what they know to be evil. Certainly, in that light, Aquinas' restrictions make sense.

The same perspective holds for the restrictions mentioned in article 10. However, some readers may note a problem. In article 10, Aquinas talks about unbelievers being led to despise the faith because of an acquaintance with the faults of Christians. This description suggests that unbelievers do not initially despise the faith, and so by *unbelievers* Aquinas could not mean sinners, as I have argued. Yet, in light of the previous context-setting discussion of unbelief as a sin, all Aquinas need mean here at article 10 is that the faults of Christians give sinners more material to despise the faith and disparage it to others.

Finally, Hood misconstrues Aquinas' words about disputations. Aquinas is not giving instructions on how to control a disputation. Aquinas is simply telling his fellow Christians that "to dispute" does not mean that one must put one's faith in doubt. As any student of medieval philosophy knows,[91] the very structure of a disputation into objections, response, and replies guarantees a thorough and fair airing of an issue. To enter an honest disputation, neither party has to reject its faith. The structure itself of the disputation establishes the intellectual honesty. If one cannot handle the disputation, one withdraws and is silent until one has something to say.

In conclusion, Hood's presentation of Aquinas on the Jews does nothing to disturb the tolerance existing between all persons of goodwill in Aquinas' social philosophy. Despite Hood's reading to the contrary, Aquinas is not speaking of all Jews. Aquinas' focus is only upon Jews guilty of the sin of unbelief.

NOTES:

[1] Epicurus, "Letter to Menoeceus" In Diogenes Laertius, *Lives and Opinions of Eminent Philosophers*, bk. XXII; trans. and ed. by A. Robert Caponigii, *Diogenes Laertius Lives of the Philosophers* (Chicago: Henry Regnery Company, 1969), 220–221.

[2] John Stuart Mill, *Utilitarianism* (Indianapolis: Bobbs-Merrill, 1957), 50–51. Likewise, ". . . but also that a direct impulse to promote the general good may be in every individual one of the habitual motives of action, and the sentiments connected therewith may fill a large and prominent place in every human being's *sentient* existence." Emphasis mine.

[3] Ibid., 49.

[4] Ibid.

[5] Ibid., 11–12.

[6] Ibid., 12.

[7] Ibid., 12–13.

[8] Ibid, 21

[9] Ibid.

[10] "Autonomy of the will is the property of the will by which it is a law to itself (independently of any property of the objects of volition)." Immanuel Kant, *Groundwork of the Metaphysics of Morals* II (German Academy ed., vol. 4, p. 440); trans. by Mary Gregor (Cambridge: Cambridge University Press, 1998), 47.

[11] "Only what is connected with my will merely as ground and never as effect, . . . —

hence the mere law for itself—can be an object of respect and so a command. Now, an action from duty is to put aside entirely the influence of inclination and with it every object of the will: hence there is left for the will nothing that could determine it except objectively the *law* and subjectively *pure respect* for this practical law, and so the maxim of complying with such a law even if it infringes upon all my inclination." Ibid, 13–14. Earlier, Kant had subsumed the good will within the notion of duty: "In order to do so [i.e., develop the notion of a good will], we shall set before ourselves the concept of duty which contains that of a good will . . . ." Ibid., 10.

¹² "But what kind of law can that be, the representation of which must determine the will, even without regard for the effect expected from it in order for the will to be called good absolutely and without limitation? . . . Nothing is left but the conformity of actions as such with universal law, which alone is to serve the will as its principle, that is, *I ought never to act except in such a way that I could also will that my maxim should become a universal law.*" Ibid., 14–15.

¹³ "This principle is, accordingly, also its supreme law: act always on that maxim whose universality as a law you can at the same time will; this is the sole condition under which a will can never be in conflict with itself, and such an imperative is categorical." Ibid., 44.

¹⁴ "For, to say that in the use of means to any end I am to limit my maxim to the condition of its universal validity as a law for every subject is tantamount to saying that the subject of ends, that is, the rational being itself, must be made the basis of all maxims of actions, never merely as a means but as the supreme limiting condition in the use of all means, that is, always at the same time as an end." Ibid., 45.

¹⁵ "Now, from this it follows incontestably that every rational being, as an end in itself, must be able to regard himself as also giving universal laws with respect to any law whatsoever to which he may be subject." Ibid., 45.

¹⁶ "Autonomy of the will is the property of the will by which it is a law to itself (independently of any property of the objects of volition)." Ibid., 47.

¹⁷ "If the will seeks the law that is to determine it anywhere else than in the fitness of its maxims for its own giving of universal law—consequently if, in going beyond itself, it seeks this law in a property of any of its objects—*heteronomy* always results. The will in that case does not give itself the law." Ibid., 47.

¹⁸ *Supra*, n. 13.

¹⁹ *Supra*, n. 17.

²⁰ *Supra*, n. 15.

²¹ This same difficulty would seem to apply to John Rawls, who in his *A Theory of Justice* (Cambridge, MA: Harvard University Press, 1971) says, "Another way of putting this is to say that the principles of justice manifest in the basic structure of society men's desire to treat one another not as means only but as ends in themselves. I cannot examine Kant's view here" (p. 179). Also, "The original position may be viewed, then, as a procedural interpretation of Kant's conception of autonomy and the categorical imperative" (p. 256). Nevertheless, this difficulty could be considered as a further basis for Rorty's recharacterization of Rawls as Deweyan, not neo-Kantian. As Deweyan, "*A Theory of Justice* no longer seems committed to a philosophical account of the human self, but only to a historico-sociological description of the way we live now." Richard Rorty, "The Priority of Democracy to Philosophy," edited in *Objectivity, Relativism, and Truth* (Cambridge: Cambridge University Press, 1991), 185.

²² Trans. by Vernon J. Bourke (Notre Dame, IN: University of Notre Dame Press, 1975), 115. In the opening line of the next argument, Aquinas makes plain that his first

argument has been thinking of the intellectual creature as free: "One who holds dominion over his own acts is free in his activity."

[23] *Supra*, n. 15.

[24] "But that the above principle of autonomy is the sole principle of morals can well be shown by mere analysis of the concepts of morality. For, by this analysis we find that its principle must be a categorical imperative, while this commands neither more nor less than just this autonomy." Kant, *Groundwork*, 47.

[25] Bourke, trans., 116–117.

[26] *De Veritate* I, 1c; XXI, 1c.

[27] *Summa Theologiae* I, 14, 1c.

[28] John Rawls, *Political Liberalism* (New York: Columbia University Press, 1993), 2.

[29] Ibid., 5–6.

[30] Ibid., 309

[31] Ibid., 10.

[32] Ibid., 48.

[33] Ibid., 61

[34] Ibid., 61–62

[35] Ibid., 19

[36] Ibid., 311.

[37] Ibid., 312–313.

[38] Ibid., 314

[39] Ibid.

[40] Ibid., 317.

[41] Ibid.

[42] Ibid., 319.

[43] Ibid., 318.

[44] Ibid.

[45] Ibid., 319.

[46] Ibid., 322.

[47] Ibid., 311.

[48] Ibid., xxiii.

[49] Ibid., xxvi

[50] Interestingly, John Courtney Murray refers to the two articles of the First Amendment of the U. S. Constitution—that is, articles on the free exercise of religion and on the non-establishment of religion—as "articles of peace." According to David L. Schindler, *Heart of the World, Center of the Church: Communion Ecclesiology, Liberalism, and Liberation* (Grand Rapids, MI: Eerdmans, 1996), 62–63, Murray's positive backup of these articles goes no further than man's autonomy—that is, man's exigency to act on his own initiative and on his own responsibility. Likewise, Schindler quotes Michael Novak: "But Murray did not think it wise to define religious liberty in terms of a philosophy and theology of the person, however profound. (For what would happen when some, inevitably, refused to accept that philosophy or theology?) Religious liberty, he believed, is a civil arrangement worked out in political history . . . rather than a deduction from rationalist premises" (73, n. 22). In other words, it appears that Murray does not go beyond Rawls and so exposes himself to Rawls' problems about which I speak. Schindler's difficulty with the logic of Murray's position on the First Amendment is a perceived fundamental indifference of the political to the religious so that the religious is simply juxtaposed to the public (p. 78). Schindler seems to be casting Murray as a proponent of Cajetan's pure nature position as it

was criticized by de Lubac for its implication of the extrinsicism of nature to grace. For more on this latter topic and on Schindler himself, see *infra* chapter VI, sec. 7. In sum, by my use of Aquinas' metaphysics (in my opinion, a necessary use if one is to establish tolerance), I am in disagreement with the political thinking of such neoconservatives as Novak. Yet because I understand that metaphysics to be the result of an a posteriori epistemology, I am in disagreement with Schindler. As I explained in chap. III, sec. 2, Aquinas understands human nature to be radically oriented to God in virtue of its ability to spontaneously and automatically abstract the *ratio entis*.

[51] Rawls, *Political Liberalism*.

[52] Ibid., 199.

[53] Ibid., 200.

[54] Ibid., 284.

[55] John Dewey, *Reconstruction in Philosophy* (Boston: Beacon Press, 1968), 37.

[56] Of course, Rorty does not share Rawls' sense of freedom of choice. For Rorty, genuine novelty is "compatible with a bleakly mechanical description of the relation between human beings and the rest of the universe." Richard Rorty, *Contingency, Irony, and Solidarity* (Cambridge: Cambridge University Press, 1989), 17. He also writes, "The ideal liberal community will be one in which respect for such particularity and idiosyncrasy is widespread, one in which the only sort of human liberty that is hoped for is Isaiah Berlin's 'negative liberty'—being left alone." "Habermas, Derrida, and Philosophy," edited in *Truth and Progress: Philosophical Papers* (Cambridge: Cambridge University Press, 1998), vol. 3, p. 322. Rorty takes no notice of a clash between mechanism and novelty.

[57] Richard Rorty, "On Ethnocentrism: A Reply to Clifford Geertz," edited in *Objectivity, Relativism, and Truth* (Cambridge: Cambridge University Press, 1991), 206.

[58] Ibid., 207.

[59] Richard Rorty, "Feminism and Pragmatism," edited in *Truth and Progress,* 205, n. 8.

[60] Ibid., 172.

[61] Richard Rorty, "Human Rights, Rationality, and Sentimentality," in *Truth and Progress: Philosophical Papers,* vol. 3, p. 181.

[62] Ibid., 180.

[63] Ibid., 185. For further discussion of this genre of literature, see Rorty's discussion of Orwell in chapter 8 of Rorty's *Contingency, Irony, and Solidarity* (Cambridge: Cambridge University Press, 1989).

[64] Rorty, "Human Rights, Rationality, and Sentimentality," 181.

[65] Ibid., 182.

[66] For Rorty, reality is too faceless to privilege any one vocabulary. For a discussion of his reasons, see my "Incommensurability and Aquinas' Metaphysics," *Proceedings of the American Catholic Philosophical Association* 65 (1991), 179–190.

[67] David Hume, *A Treatise of Human Nature*, bk. III, pt. III, sec. 1; Green and Grose eds., *David Hume: The Philosophical Works* (Darmstadt: Scientia Verlag Aalen, 1964), vol. 2, pp. 335–336.

[68] *Summa Contra Gentiles* III, 26; Bourke trans., *Summa Contra Gentiles*, III, 105

[69] *Summa Theologiae* II-II, 10, 1 and 5.

[70] "We must now consider the good and evil of human acts. First, how a human act is good or evil; secondly, what results from the good or evil of a human act, as merit or demerit, sin and guilt." *Summa Theologiae* I-II, 18, intro; trans. English Dominican Fathers, *Summa Theologica* (New York: Benziger Brothers, 1947) I, 662.

[71] "And since those acts are properly called human, which are voluntary, because the will is the rational appetite, which is proper to man." *Summa Theologiae* I-II, 6, introduction; English Dominican Fathers, *Summa Theologica* I, 615. "As stated above (a. 1), it is essential to the voluntary act that its principle be within the agent together with some knowledge of the end." *Summa Theologiae* I-II, 6, 2c; English Dominican Fathers, *Summa Theologica* I, 617.

[72] *The New Catholic Encyclopedia* calls such heresy "formal heresy" as distinct from "material heresy." It defines formal heresy as a baptized person and retaining the name of Christian who "pertinaciously denies or doubts any of the truths that one is under obligation of divine and Catholic faith to believe." (New York: McGraw-Hill, 1967), 6, 1069. *Pertinaciously* means that "despite certainty that such or such a truth is of the Catholic faith, the heretic with culpable obstinacy refuses to assent to it." Congruent with my interpretation of Aquinas, *The New Catholic Encyclopedia* remarks (p. 1063), "The medieval scholastics, with their optimistic view of the powers of human reason to achieve the truth, took a correspondingly poor view, morally speaking, of any error, especially heresy. Hence the conviction, long dominant, that heresy's fellow is bad faith; and it was a long while before heresy was reckoned as falling within the ambit of inculpable error."

[73] "Some have understood the authority quoted to forbid, not the excommunication but the slaying of heretics, as appears from the words of Chrysostom. Augustine too, says (*Ep. Ad Vincent.* xciii) of himself: *It was once my opinion that none should be compelled to union with Christ, that we should deal in words and fight with arguments. However, this opinion of mine is undone, not by words of contradiction, but by convincing examples. Because fear of the law was so profitable, that many say: Thanks be to the Lord Who has broken our chains asunder.* Accordingly the meaning of Our Lord's words, *Suffer both to grow until the harvest,* must be gathered from those which precede, *lest perhaps gathering up the cockle, you root up the wheat also together with it.* For Augustine says (*Contra Ep. Parmen.* iii 2) *these words show that when this is not to be feared, that is to say, when a man's crime is so publicly known, and so hateful to all, that he has no defenders, or none such as might cause a schism, the severity of the discipline should not slacken.*" *Summa Theologiae* II-II, 10, 8, ad 1m; English Dominican Fathers trans., *Summa Theologica* II, 1219.

[74] "For, since the sin of unbelief consists in resisting the faith, this may happen in two ways: either the faith is resisted before it has been accepted, and such is the unbelief of pagans or heathens; or the Christian faith is resisted after it has been accepted, and this either in figure, and such is the unbelief of the Jews, or in the very manifestation of truth, and such is the unbelief of heretics." *Summa Theologiae* II-II, 10, 5; English Dominican Fathers trans., *Summa Theologica* II, 1216.

[75] John Y. B. Hood, *Aquinas and the Jews* (Philadelphia: University of Pennsylvania Press, 1995).

[76] Ibid., 92.

[77] Ibid., 87. Although the medieval Church considered Jews to be a danger and acted accordingly, the Church seemingly is not considering Jews in that same light as Aquinas. As Hood describes it (pp. 70–84), the target of Church reaction was Jews who had honest intellectual disagreements with the Christian faith. Aquinas does not cast his net so widely. Aquinas considers only those Jews guilty of the sin of unbelief.

[78] Ibid., 86.

[79] Also, see Hood's listing of Jewish intellectual problems with Christianity on pp. 82–83.

[80] Hood, *Aquinas and the Jews*, 87. Likewise, Steven Boguslawski, *Thomas Aquinas on the Jews* (New York: Paulist Press, 2008), 36: "Thomas does not conceive of the Jews as an undifferentiated social group. With regard to responsibility for the crucifixion, for example, he distinguishes subgroups within Judaism, absolving the majority common folk and blaming the leadership." Boguslawski cites *Summa Theologiae* III, 47, 5.

[81] "Just as taking a vow is a matter of will, and keeping a vow, a matter of obligation, so acceptance of the faith is a matter of the will, whereas keeping the faith, when once one has received it, is a matter of obligation. Wherefore heretics should be compelled to keep the faith." *Summa Theologiae* II-II, 10, 8, ad 3m; English Dominican Fathers trans., *Summa Theologica* II, 1219. Usually, obligation is a matter of the practical intellect and is *followed* by an act of will. See *Summa Theologiae* I-II, 94, 2c, on the first principle of practical reason. But in the preceding quote, Aquinas is speaking specifically of obligation to keep a vow. Here, obligation *presupposes* the act of will that is the taking of the vow. Hence, in compelling the heretic, there is no violation of his will.

[82] Aquinas, *Summa Theologiae* II-II, 10, 8c.

[83] Aquinas, *Summa Theologiae* II-II, 10, 12c.

[84] Hood, *Aquinas and the Jews*, p. 92. Hood also writes (p. 90), "Aquinas in effect argues that it is better to allow a child to suffer eternal torment than to violate natural justice."

[85] For a collection of Thomistic texts on the state of unbaptized children after death and for a commentary, see William R. O'Connor, *The Eternal Quest: The Teaching of St. Thomas Aquinas on the Natural Desire for God* (New York: Longmans, Green, 1947), 191–196.

[86] "Thus from the fact that the Jews observe their rites, which, of old, foreshadowed the truth of the faith which we hold, there follows this good—that our very enemies bear witness to our faith, and that our faith is represented in figure, so to speak." Dominican Fathers trans., *Summa Theologica* II, 1222.

[87] Hood, *Aquinas and the Jews*, 94.

[88] Ibid.

[89] Ibid., 97.

[90] "One ought to dispute about matters of faith, not as though one doubted about them, but in order to make the truth known, and to confute errors." Aquinas, *Summa Theologiae* II-II, 10, 7, ad 3m; Dominican Fathers trans., *Summa Theologica* II, 1218.

[91] See Armand A. Maurer, *Medieval Philosophy* (New York: Random House, 1965), 91.

VI
Cultural Pluralism

1. The Challenge of Westernization

I once met a Lithuanian professor of ethnology from the University of Vilnius. In reply to my questions about his experience of living during Soviet times, he provided a recently published autobiographical article. In the article, Prof. Čiubrinskas notes that the Soviets attacked the identity of the Lithuanian people by attacking their language and their religion. He says,

> The third idea promoted by Brezhnev in the 1970s was "the new historical community": the creation of the Soviet people as a consequence of the "mature socialism" achieved in the Soviet Union. Thus, the invention of a "super-modern" type of society, more advanced than the nation-state, was proclaimed. This was said to be a "monolithically united community" which had already overcome "the national question" by eliminating all the social and most of the cultural differences among the nations within the Soviet Union. The new community would be brought about by the introduction of Russian as the lingua franca and then imposing total linguistic Russification. From the late 1970s, Moscow initiated a series of policies aimed at greater cultural standardization. These included the decree that Russian be taught in kindergartens, schools, and universities. Such policies did much to heighten concern over the future of the local language and culture. . . . Administration, communication and accounting in virtually all institutions was carried out in the language of "Big Brother." This constituted a serious challenge to one of the most powerful sources of Lithuanian pride and identity, "the unique and ancient Lithuanian language."
>
> Another cornerstone of "the new community" was the aggressive imposition of atheism. The Criminal Code declared "the

organization and systematic teaching of religion to minors to be a criminal act"; . . . the public sphere was totally closed to religious and church life. Part of the Church was driven underground (convents, even entire orders, not to speak of religious teaching, were suppressed). . . . Dozens of churches were converted into public buildings, and thousands of folk-art monuments, particularly wayside crosses, were destroyed "as signs of religious propaganda." Of course the Lithuanians, who had not been exposed to modern secularization and had no institutions such as civil marriage until the Soviet occupation, were shocked by this policy, which undermined a fundamental tenet of their national identity: being "a proper Lithuanian" meant to be a Roman Catholic. The result was that, by the 1970s, two thirds of all manifestations of dissent in Lithuania were of a religious nature, and only one-third dealt with the topic of national rights. . . . The largest underground periodical publication in Eastern Europe, the *Chronicle of the Catholic Church of Lithuania*, focused exclusively on the suppression of religion.

So the core of Lithuanian national culture—language and religion—had been threatened into virtual disappearance from public life. There was almost no room left for them in the new historical community.[1]

Čiubrinskas goes on to describe the various strategies that Lithuanians developed to protect this core of national culture. But what is especially poignant to me is his autobiographical conclusion.

By the 1990s, I had shifted from an essentialist and ascriptive approach to the question of identity to a more critical view of "constructed" identity.

This deconstruction of my original "Baltophile," folklore-orientated, nationalist view of identity and the move to a more critical and individual vision, took a long time to happen. . . .

One thing is certain, the change was "programmed" by my personal development and, to a large extent, by my numerous and extensive periods of study at Western universities. . . . That I have had access to Western scholarly books, which had been almost prohibited during the Soviet period, and to modern scholarly discourses on national identity and nationalism has undoubtedly influenced and eventually changed my perspective on my own national identity. Finally, my new perspective on the concept of identity fits well into the framework of post-Communist academic life at my university in Vilnius. But it remains inimical to the numerous institutions, social networks, and even politicians still engaged in the revival of ethnic culture and confronting a new enemy now—Americanization and globalization.[2]

Čiubrinskas mentions that the deconstruction of his Baltophile identity was programmed by his study of Western books on national identity. Undoubtedly involved here is familiarity with Benedict Anderson's reflections on nationalism.[3] For Anderson, national identity is an ephemeral product of the printing industry that is exploited and manipulated by the power or would-be power elites. So, for example, previous talk about Lithuania's glorious past as a nation and its ancient language turn out to be fictions that a small group, usually of bourgeois character, uses to manipulate society to throw off Czarist domination. National identity has no deep grounding in truth. Rather, its basis lies simply in the game of acquiring power. With its deprecation of nationalism and its emphasis on the dynamics of print-capitalism, Anderson's work might be described as neo-Marxist. That quality might explain Anderson's grip over Čiubrinskas and his colleagues.[4] Yet the problem of preserving a Baltophile identity has a more profound source than current academic research by former Soviet Lithuanians.

Those entering the West encounter this argument: to be Western is to be democratic, but to be democratic one must profess tolerance, and tolerance means the exclusion of characteristic claims in regard to religion, nation, culture, philosophy, and so on. As I explained in chapter I, behind this thinking is the skepticism defense of tolerance and its fear that truth is tyrannical. We will all get along if we all realize that no one can ever claim to possess the truth. And so, to enter the West, Lithuania (and, obviously, other countries, too) must pay the price of neutering itself religiously and culturally. What the Soviets could not eradicate, the West is eradicating. What, during Soviet times, was so dear and precious to Lithuanians is now characterized as fictions used to manipulate.

In this chapter, I would like to extend my reflections on Aquinas' natural law as a basis for tolerance to Aquinas' natural law as a basis for cultural identity. As absolute as the truth of Aquinas' natural law ethics is, the third section in this chapter will show that Aquinas' use of analogical understanding of the moral good presents the possibility of a morally legitimate flowering of cultures. In the fourth section, I take advantage of Dawson's anthropological analysis of the rise and fall of cultures through history to illustrate more concretely the predominance of Aquinas' moral psychology. De facto cultural pluralism is no objection to the omnipresence of Aquinas' psychology of the human as an intellector of being.

2. Catholicism and Cultural Pluralism

Can the process of Westernization be halted without becoming anti-democratic—without morphing into fascism? To avoid the latter, must one come to regard one's cultural identity not as something deep and precious, but as something cheap and mundane? For two reasons, I believe that the process can be stopped and that something like fascism can be avoided. First, the above argument skips a beat in its claim that tolerance excludes characteristic claims because tolerance must be based on skepticism. For example, a Catholic can insist that, for theological reasons, Catholicism embraces tolerance, not just in the sense of mutual noninterference but in the sense of fraternity. As the Vatican II document *Gaudium et Spes* (*The Church in the Modern World*) succinctly explains (at paragraph 24), because God as Father has called all of us to Himself, then we are all brothers and sisters and should treat ourselves accordingly. So, in its religious heritage, any Catholic country has a better reason than skepticism for the tolerance so treasured by current Western democracy.

But my suggestion raises a question. Supposedly I am defending a national identity, but what I have just defended is a Catholic identity. So, for example, though a Lithuanian may be a Catholic, a Catholic does not have to be a Lithuanian. In fact, I have heard it argued that, like Westernization and globalization, Catholicism is inimical to a national and ethnic identity. This logical gap in my thesis requires going deeper into the brotherly love to which the faith impels us. In a word, this love is analogous.

Consider again sanctity among the saints. Christian holiness assumes a wild and crazy array of analogates that defies stereotyping. Just when we think that we have seen all that there is to sanctity, a new and different way of doing the same emerges. In Augustine's time, a Christian would have already known Christian heroes. But could that Christian have envisaged a Bonaventure, Francis, Benedict, Ignatius, or Therese of Lisieux? Today, after centuries, we are in the same situation. Sanctity, or brotherly love, continually bursts stereotyping.

Obviously, such a religious system does not entail a Lithuanian identity just as it does not entail a Jesuit, Franciscan, Carmelite, or Benedictine identity. But such a system permits and encourages all of these. In a word, within Catholicism, an entire people can find a refuge for an identity. Just as Bonaventure found his unique way of being a saint within Catholicism, an entire people can do the same. Was this not the case in the drive for Lithuania's first independence in the last century? Clerics and lay people saw that there was a Lithuanian way of being a Catholic, not just the Polish way. Their realization of this analogate led to the Lithuanian nation. So, in conclusion, if Catholics are mindful of their religious heritage, they should remember the analogous character of holiness and be the most respectful of people. In that way also, an ethnicity should merit, from others, tolerance for its own identity.

3. Aquinas' Thought and Cultural Pluralism

So that is the first answer. The second answer follows the question, "Is any present country sufficiently Catholic to take advantage of this deep source of identity?" For example, is Lithuania still a Catholic country—a country whose citizens are guided by Catholic mores and beliefs? Can Lithuania appeal to its Catholicism now as easily as it did during its previous independence? Between then and now was almost fifty years of Soviet atheist ideology. Has that not had an effect both on the intelligentsia and the people? I have traveled to Lithuania many times and have had good exposure both to students and professors. The general attitude that I find is that if you want to philosophize, you do not go to a Catholic thinker like Aquinas but to a non-Catholic like Kant or Husserl or Russell. Catholic thinkers are members of an authoritatively teaching Church and so cannot be trusted to do honest philosophy.

As an aside, let me say that this attitude must be branded for what it is, namely crass ad hominem reasoning unbefitting professional academics. Ad hominem reasoning criticizes what is said simply on the basis of the one saying it. And so I guess that we would have to doubt that 2+2=4 simply because the Pope uttered it. No, religious people can also philosophize. Hopefully I have illustrated this point in the case of the theologian Aquinas and the philosophical worth of his ideas for ethics and for social and political philosophy. Aquinas is as good a philosopher as Kant, Husserl, Russell, or Heidegger are thought by many to be.

But you do not have to trust my observations of the Lithuanian academic scene. Čiubrinskas himself notes the current predominant attitude of Western skepticism among his fellow academics at Vilnius University. As he concluded, "Finally, my new perspective on the concept of identity fits well into the framework of post-Communist academic life at my university in Vilnius. But it remains inimical to the numerous institutions, social networks, and even politicians still engaged in the revival of ethnic culture and confronting a new enemy now—Americanization and globalization." What Čiubrinskas is talking about as his new concept of identity is the postmodern attitude that identity is a voluntaristic phenomenon and so is anything that you, or the power elites, want it to be. In short, Čiubrinskas and his colleagues are exactly in the dilemma that I sketched in chapter I—we defend tolerance by skepticism. But then we have no logical defense against someone who decides to be intolerant. But I do not want to be unfair to my Lithuanian colleagues. One can also wonder about the Catholic commitment of politicians and business leaders. If Lithuanians really lived their faith, they would treat themselves as brothers and sisters. Do they? Has not independence meant money for the few and poverty for the many?

Given the disaffection with Catholicism among leading portions of national populations, I do not think that one can just appeal to people to turn to their Catholicism to resist the acid bath of Westernization. Not enough people believe in Catholicism to make the appeal effective. I know a few religiously minded academics who are pleased by a situation in which unbelievers precipitate into a pool of skepticism. These thinkers follow Kant's strategy of denying reason to make room for faith. The more defeated the unbeliever is, the more the unbeliever will submit to religion. This type of thinking generates theocracies and ayatollahs; it has no pedigree in Catholicism for which grace builds on nature.

And so I come to my second answer to the question, "Can a country resist the neutering effects of Westernization without becoming intolerant?" This question expresses a problem that by its nature is philosophical. It is the problem of truth and tolerance. As a philosophical problem, it requires a philosophical solution. It will do no good to hit a philosophical problem with a theological club. That is why the ethics of Aquinas and its accommodation of a strong sense of tolerance are so valuable. To the philosophical problem of truth and tolerance, Aquinas offers a philosophical solution. Aquinas' ethical principles do not presuppose his religious beliefs, and so they speak to everyone of goodwill. People may stop being Catholic and they may stop being reasonable, but they usually do the first before doing the second. Aquinas' philosophical thinking is there to catch them at that point.

A citizenry that accommodates tolerance through the truth of

Aquinas' natural law ethics can maintain a cultural identity in a way similar to the Catholic citizenry described above. Though Aquinas' ethics does not entail a specific national and cultural identity, his ethics permits and encourages it. Just as the moral response of individuals will generate specific identities—the fisherman for a caring father in the Pacific islands and the hunter for such a father in Siberia—so, too, groups of people can do the same. Consider how, out of concern for their families, mothers discovered and shared ideas not only for the most nutritional food in their time and place but also for the most pleasing, not only for the most protective clothing but the most attractive. Is it difficult to extrapolate these two things into a particular ethnic cuisine and a particular ethnic dress and with other similar things, like music and art, into an entire culture?

And so, in Aquinas' ethics, a people is presented with the task and inspiration to craft a culture for the time and place in which they live.[5] Through the respect owing to our fellows as intellectors of being, Aquinas' ethics, in a way similar to the previously noted call to holiness, generates new analogates of morally good living. Fidelity to the intuition of being is the key. In some way, either implicitly or explicitly, a people must be guided by this intuition. If they are, they will find *ipso facto* that they have formed a distinctive identity. Being will have given such a populace the gift of a culture. In sum, identity has its source in morality, and morality has its source in the analogon of being.

Also, as explained in chapter V, Aquinas' ethics openly proclaims self-correcting grounds for fixing any intolerance into which the society might slip. The responsibility of the state is not to settle philosophical problems but to protect the common good through its legislation. So the state can act in regard to philosophies only when their most threatening practical implications come to bear on the common good. Hence, the social minorities should not fear the ethnic majority and its possible control of the government. Likewise, from the Thomistic perspective, the ethnic majority of that country should also be able to exercise its preferences without accusations of tyranny. Just as the majority is taught to respect the minority, so too, the minority can be taught to respect the majority and its cultural preferences. Hence, state occasions need not be conducted in business suits but can be in traditional ethnic costumes. These cultural practices have nothing to do with the majority excluding the nonethnic minority. The social and political implications of Aquinas' ethics are already there to guarantee a place in society for the minority. Rather, the practices have everything to do with the majority celebrating its customs. Also, just as a good transportation network is part of the common good, there is no doubt that a single language is to the benefit of society's common good. Imposition of the language has nothing to do with an exercise of cultural imperialism; rather, it has everything to do with a smoothly running society. So, in being asked to learn the language of the majority, the nonnative speakers of the minority are not being asked to give up their cultural heritage, and discrimination on that basis would be against the fraternity that basically marks the common good.

The Thomistic moral basis of culture is also dynamic. Cultures will need to change and even to assimilate. As I will show, Christopher Dawson provides a keenly observant narrative of cultural history. The narrative illustrates that culture has always been morally based. That moral basis illuminates why people can be so recalcitrant to cultural change. In their eyes, change means infidelity to the sacrifices of those that came before. But just as I said that, in speculative matters, diamond must cut diamond, here moral demands must meet moral demands. Acting by the same moral principles that guided one's forebears assuages the pain in surrendering time-honored cultural practices. That is the genuine way to respect one's ancestors. Respect and solicitude for the living person is what is primary. Such obligation generates both culture and cultural change.

Finally and hopefully, the recognition of Aquinas' philosophical ideas may lead the intellectuals of a Catholic country to reconsider its religious heritage. As a student is helped to learn mathematics by using a book with answers at the back, so too, Aquinas was assisted in his philosophizing by his faith. This methodology provided Aquinas with indications of where the philosophical truth may lie, but it left Aquinas with the demanding work of discovering the philosophical analyses and arguments. Many consider this procedure a bias, and I acknowledge that it can be abused. But in Aquinas' hands, are not its advantages evident?

As mentioned, Aquinas alone seems to have philosophically grounded an ethics that has the logical room for the current desideratum of the common good—tolerance. Does not this success, and there are others, not cause to cross one's mind the thought that just maybe there is something to the Catholic faith. The success of Aquinas' philosophy urges us to consider the higher light that encouraged it. But, even if intellectuals reclaimed their religious heritage, Aquinas' philosophical ideas would not become superfluous. Again, if God has called all of us to Himself as Father, then we are all brothers and sisters. A Catholic country's going West would involve the task of offering, in respectful dialogue, Aquinas' solution to the philosophical problem of truth and tolerance. In the brotherly love to which religion calls us may be the burden of offering philosophical aid to our fellows. Given the needs of others, the Good Samaritan can assume many different forms at different times.

4. Dawson's Cultural Anthropology and Aquinas' Philosophical Psychology

Like my presentation of natural law in chapter II, my explanation of cultural identity in terms of morality may seem too naive to be true. Rather than morality, crass economic interests or desires for domination explain the rise and fall of cultures. This criticism returns us to the battlefield of philosophical psychology. I will remind the reader of Aquinas' philosophical case that being haunts the human mind. Being is there when we are moral; being is there when we are immoral. Also, in chapter IV, I explained how Aquinas' psychology can defend itself against a hedonistic psychology, such as Mill's, a transcendental psychology, such as Kant's, and a "free-standing" political view, such as Rawls', and can appropriate the best features of all of these. Hence, I could simply insist that, appearances to the contrary, my basing cultural identity on a morality of natural law is neither a pipe dream nor wishful thinking, for the basis in reality of Aquinas' natural law position has been verified.

But just as I went on to explain how an intellector of being and the good could do evil and be confused about self-evident precepts of natural law, it would be useful to shine the light of Thomistic psychology on cultural history. If being haunts the human mind, being should also haunt cultural history. For this survey of cultural history, I will take advantage of Christopher Dawson's work in cultural anthropology. As I summarize his narrative, I will interject remarks from Aquinas' psychological perspective. I hope to illustrate that a moral basis for cultural identity is not too distant from the actual history of cultures. Cultures have always been a response to the intellection of being. Instead of calling us to a place that we have never been, the moral basis for culture is calling us home.

Accordingly, I see Richard Rorty's thesis of the priority of democracy over philosophy as too narrowly defined.[6] By *philosophy* Rorty means explicit philosophy, philosophy done by philosophers. But before that, and due to the spontaneous workings of the human mind, an implicit philosophy exists in every human. Further, Rorty's claim that only history and sociology—not the discipline of philosophical anthropology—are required as a preface to politics[7] draws a too facile distinction between philosophy and history/sociology. Human experience is never just history; it has always included intellection.

To introduce Dawson, I would like to review some points and to note an implication of them. As I said in chapter III, although Aquinas regards the primary precepts as self-evident to us, such knowledge is implicit long before it is raised to consciousness. Aquinas' abstractionist epistemology explains this position. Though the intellect has gone on to abstract the *ratio entis*, one's attention can linger on the data. Also, because one's attention is focused more on the sensible data than on data from subjectivity, then even when the fruits of intellection are appreciated, one can still miss the dignity of the human person. These facts of Thomistic psychology ought to entail for natural law a development in human history.

The general lines of this historical unfolding should be as follows. Moral obligation should first arise in respect to objective phenomena. These phenomena should be the large or the small whose consideration demands the presence of the *ratio entis*. Since the *ratio entis* harbors causal implications, the causal implications of the *ratio entis* could be confused with the phenomenon itself. Moreover, since the causal implications instantiate the *ratio essendi*, the key component in the *ratio entis*, then the causal implications will be a heightened presentation of the good and call forth an obligatory respect and solicitude. Hence, the beginnings of cultural development should be reflected in cosmological morality. Only later, with the reflective (and probably implicit) discernment of the human person as an intellector of being, would a personalist morality emerge.[8] Even though these two epiphanies of the *ratio entis*—namely, the creator and the human—are found in Aquinas' natural law ethics, one can suspect that striking the correct integration of and ordering between these two sources of morality would be naturally achieved, if ever, only after wild swings and oscillations between them. One can be so intent upon the worldly data as real that one never appreciates the awesome fact of the cognitional existence of the *ratio entis*. Likewise, as is evident from my philosophical unfolding of the content of *Summa Theologiae* I-II, 94, 2c, one can come to know oneself as an intellector of being before the reduction of being to a first cause that is subsistent *esse*.

So, one can suspect that a cosmological morality and a personalist morality are two poles that will mark the swings of cultural history. A balanced position would be rare and short-lived. I want to attempt to illustrate the truth of these expectations by relating Aquinas' psychology to Christopher Dawson's work in cultural anthropology. I believe that his observations dovetail with Aquinas' psychology. By interspersing Thomistic remarks with a summary of Dawson's narration of the history of cultural development in his *Progress and Religion*,[9] I hope to show the possibility of a Thomistic philosophy of culture.

a. Dawson on archaic religion. By *culture*, Dawson understands a way of life of a particular people adapted to a special environment.[10] Culture is the result of an intimate communion between man and the region in which and from which he lives. Nevertheless, culture is not a mere passive result of material forces. The greatest agent of cultural development is the human intellect. By *intellect*, Dawson does not understand the human mind of modern science but the "whole domain of human consciousness from the first obscure effort to correlate the data of sensible experience up to the highest achievements of the speculative intellect."[11] In respect to this wider sense of intellect, Dawson introduces the *religious impulse* or *intuition*.[12] The religious impulse places man under something that is transcendent and to which he owes allegiance. It is the dynamic element for cultural development. In primitive cultures, the religious impulse consists in an obscure and confused intuition of transcendent or pure being. The object of intuition is variously referred to. It is the Wakan of the Dakota Indians, Cagn for the Australian Bushmen, Yok for the Eskimos. None of these references is to be confused with the more obvious mythologies of these primitive cultures. The superficial and ridiculous elements of the mythologies can camouflage the depth and reality of the religious dimension of the cultures.[13]

Dawson's observations dovetail with Aquinas' thoughts on a pre-philosophical knowledge of God and its implicit metaphysical character. For Dawson, the anthropological facts illustrate that the human is never so primitive as to lack intellectual capacity. Hence, as the primitive human looks out at the world, that intellectual capacity introduces him to a transcendent being. For Aquinas, the intellectual capacity is defined by its object, the *ratio entis*. In primitive times, the consideration of the natural world and awesome objects within it would have forced the use of this object. The causal implications embedded in the *ratio entis* would, in turn, have brought the thought of a transcendent being into the mind of the primitive.[14]

Dawson goes on to notice how cultural development follows upon the religious impulse. The intuition of transcendent being is more than an intellectual discovery like the Pythagorean theorem. The intuition is a grasp of something to which the human owes allegiance. Moreover, since the transcendent being is behind nature, there follows a human conforming to natural rhythms. In primitive cultures, elaborate rituals and ceremonies express this conformity. Dawson surmises that the religious practices were the occasions for the development of agriculture and husbandry. This observation becomes clearer in cultures with a distinct class of priests.[15] For example, a practical knowledge as to the care of seed and time and place of planting suffuses the rituals of the Pueblo Indians of Arizona and New Mexico. Mayan and Aztec cultures continue the development of culture within the womb of religion. Here the ritual cycle led to amazing progress in astronomical and chronological science. Jumping continents, the same can be observed in ancient China and India, though only vestiges survive under forms of higher culture.[16] Finally, of course, the Egypt of the pyramid builders is the paradigmatic case of an entire high civilization organized around the religious impulse—the glorification of the Sun god and his child, the god King.[17]

Dawson mentions a price paid by these archaic religions. They purchased a steadfastness by conforming themselves to the larger cycle of the natural world. Hence, human history is circular, not linear. To a Thomist, this stalemate is unsurprising. The consideration of nature can involve a heightened presentation of being, but nature is not itself an epiphany of being. That status is reserved for the human person. So, until that confusion is untangled, culture will not be able to take advantage of morality as a fount for identity. But of more interest to a Thomist is Dawson's explanation of the way cultures eventually flounder. The reef upon which cultures come to wreck is urbanization.[18] Referring to Hellenic civilization, Dawson observes that its strength was drawn from its regional and agrarian foundation. The citizen was not only a landowner but a farmer, the rough Acharnian peasant and rural Dorian noble. When the Greeks became a nation of town dwellers, its culture was in its heyday and yet falling apart from within. As Dawson sees it, one can observe the same dynamic in the passing of Roman civilization and in our industrialized societies.

Reflecting on Dawson's observations of the danger of urbanization, the Thomist will see a congruence with Aquinas' psychology. The hectic character of urban life that is often driven by a desire for power or wealth distracts attention from the world of nature whose consideration most readily calls for the *ratio entis*. But being is still there, at least implicitly, in the minds of the urban populace. Urban life then leads to a dissonance in the minds of people, a sense of futility and disrespect of oneself. Moreover, the current psychological programs that try to deal with this dissonance by emphasizing one's self-worth inevitably fail because subjectivity by itself is not the solution. As noted in Aquinas, what gives us a sense of our own self-worth is not intellection per se but the object of intellection, the *ratio entis*.

But the *ratio entis* is an abstraction, and, to be grasped, abstractions require appropriate data. Hence, to grasp our own dignity, we must grasp being in our intellection. For such a grasp to have impact, intellection must begin from appropriate data. As rulers realized at the time of Rome's decline, spectacle is an effective datum to distract us from our woes. But if spectacle succeeds in giving us a sense of being and so some sense of our own dignity as intellectors of being, then spectacle can also exacerbate feelings of hopelessness. Far from calming the populace, spectacle can agitate the populace. Better to provide sources of recreation—dissonant music, alcohol, video games, and the like—that do not so readily suggest being. Attention must be kept on the data. The ruler must eschew any possibility of the populace achieving a perception of depth to the situation.

In other words, we need to distinguish between recreation and leisure. Joseph Pieper spoke eloquently of leisure as the basis of culture, which is our current concern. Pieper connects leisure with the philosophical act of wonder, which in turn he connects to an intuition of being: "The innermost meaning of wonder is fulfilled in a deepened sense of mystery. It does not end in doubt, but is the awakening of the knowledge that being, qua being, is mysterious and inconceivable, and that it is a mystery in the full sense of the word: neither a dead end, nor a contradiction, nor even something impenetrable and dark. Rather, mystery means that a reality cannot be comprehended because its light is ever-flowing, unfathomable, and inexhaustible. And that is what the wonderer really experiences."[19]

This passage summarizes admirably what I expressed as the analogical character of the *ratio entis*. As a sameness-in-difference, the *ratio entis* is only partially revealed by its analogates. Moreover, as expressing the *ratio entis*, the differences of things are seen to arise from the *ratio entis*. Consequently, the *ratio entis* is apprehended as an unfathomable concrescence of perfection and, obviously, as an object of wonder. This view on things *sub ratione entis*, however dim or bright it may be, provides refreshment and orientation to life. Aquinas' philosophical psychology and Dawson's reflections both indicate that a sense of being is, and has been, available to ordinary people. A quiet and perhaps solitary contemplation of natural things, for example, provides being. To combat the eclipsing of being produced by urbanization, opportunities to be in natural surrounding must be aggrandized.

b. Dawson on the world religions. Dawson points out that, beginning around the third millennium BC, less civilized peoples of Indo-European stock assaulted the civilizations of the archaic religions. With the passing of the civilizations and the resulting chaos, the religious impulse assumed another guise. The transcendent became less a transcendent being and more a transcendent moral code.[20] The deeply felt impropriety of the social chaos set in relief this moral code. It asked not for external observance of ritual but for interior adhesion of the person. It surfaced in the Tao of Confucianism, in the Rta of the Rigveda, the most ancient of the sacred books of India, and in the Arta of Old Persia. In Hellenic culture, there corresponded the universal law of Dike, the Eternal Right. Dawson notes that Plato's *The Laws* is a classic expression of this.

To a Thomist, the shift to a divine law is reflective of the fact that moral necessity need not be initiated from the grasp of a transcendent being but from the grasp of ourselves as intellectors of being, also the good. This personal source of morality explains the continued presence of an obligation to propriety despite the demise of the archaic religions. The moral law continues to make a demand.

Dawson observes that this moral law was considered a reflection of a universal order that rules the universe. So, the Thomist can see that some confusion still exists about the source of this call for propriety. Yet some incipient grasp of the human person as the origin of this obligation is indicated in the Indian line of religion. This stretches from the Brahmins, to the Upanishads, to Buddhism. For Dawson,[21] this line returned to a stage of thought older than Archaic Culture and intuited once more the transcendent being that is the ultimate basis of religion. Yet the supreme principle was identified with Atman, or Self. Atman was considered to be the source of all that exists, especially our own consciousness. It was the Soul of our soul with which our soul was in a sense identical.

This subjective twist to the absolute is also understandable in Thomistic psychology. As noted in chapter III's presentation of Aquinas on the general knowledge of God had by all men, we can experience external things so large that a consideration of them forces the utilization of the *ratio entis* whose causal implications can be confused with the external thing itself. The same model can be applied to internal experience. To contemplate ourselves who intellect being, we must use being. Hence, we can confuse ourselves with the causal implications of being. We can lose our identity in the absolute.[22]

Dawson notes that the Upanishads' achievement of Atman transforms the spiritual attitude of Indian religion.[23] The moral ideal no longer has any relation to social rights and duties. True happiness is to be found in a flight from the world to unity with Atman. Though it contains less speculation than the Upanishads, Buddhism also makes deliverance primary. Buddhism is ethical by assuming a fatalistic stance in regard to life and the external world. Dawson observes a similar development in China.[24] To the propriety of a Confucian life-style, Lao Tzu preached a mystical cosmology whose ideal was one of quietism and spiritual detachment. Interestingly, Dawson observes that these fatalistic refinements of Indian and Chinese religion survived only because of the continuance among the populace of traditional archaic culture with its religion of mysterious forces in nature. A Thomist would see this fact as more than a grudging acknowledgment of practical necessity. It also expresses an epistemological one. To confuse the causal implications of being with the self, one must first have the notion of being. But as an abstraction, being requires the data of sensation. The personalist pole of morality can never eliminate the cosmological pole.

But the oriental spirit of flight from the world migrated into the Hellenic and Roman world views. Platonic mysticism used intelligence, not asceticism, to flee the world.[25] The Roman Stoics denigrated the world by understanding the world to function cyclically in imitation of the realm of pure being. As functioning cyclically, the world produces nothing new and so slips from interest.

So far in Dawson's narrative, human intelligence shows itself as unable to achieve an integral view of morality. The religious impulse began cosmologically. From that basis it generated, for example, Mayan and Egyptian cultures. But when the vagaries of history prompted attention to a personalist basis for morality, the cosmological pole became severely subservient to the personalist pole. The highest form of religion consisted in a kamikaze feat. The most holy ones left the world for an obliterating union with the absolute Self.

This triumph of personalistic morality is not surprising to a Thomist. The world may provide a heightened presence of being, but the world is not itself an epiphany of being. Only intellectors of being and certain of their actions are epiphanies of being. Hence, in any competition between the cosmological pole and the personalistic pole of morality, even an inchoate sense of human dignity will prevail every time. But winning can be pyrrhic, as was the case in the Orient. Only by keeping the world real do we guarantee the objectivity of being, which—as the good—in turn bestows dignity on its intellector. Lose the world and the *ratio entis* ceases to be a reliable guide to the location of true moral worth.

Religion was called back to its senses with Judaism.[26] Dawson observes that unlike the other world religions which were linked to some great historic culture, the religion of Israel practically lacked a material foundation. This religion belonged to a minor people, neither rich nor highly civilized, and living in a limited territory. But for Aquinas there is always in the human an intellectual base. The spontaneous and automatic abstraction of being stamps the human intellect. Hence, it is conceivable that, in certain individuals, there results an attunement to the call from the creator of the world. Being calls to the intellector of being and instant communication is achieved. Dawson also observes that Israel possessed no metaphysical tradition. But the lack does not cut against my Thomistic observation. The human intellect has a life of its own before the start of philosophy. Even at an implicit level, the life of the human intellect is luxuriant enough to positively dispose some individuals to revelation.

Now the creator of heaven and earth exercises the initiative and breaks into human history with his revelation to the Jewish people. Even though the eruption of the absolute was not in the self, revelation was a dialogue of personal creator to created person. This manner of relation established from its beginning a value to the created person by the creator of the world. Hence, in Judaism, both the world and the person have a place. This is a religion that integrates both the cosmological and personalist poles of morality, or in Dawson's terminology, both forms of the religious impulse. But the integration exists because of the divine initiative. The balance and integrity of Aquinas' natural law position is in fact a very elusive point for human reason to hit and required divine assistance to realize.

Interesting is Dawson's observation that the dialogue between creator and created persons provides Judaism with a distinctive identity as a world religion. Because persons were involved, Judaism alone saw the historical process as going somewhere. Does not the observation reiterate my point from earlier in this chapter? A morality based on respect and solicitude for the person will result in forging a distinctive cultural identity for communities.

Dawson goes on to notice that, with Christianity, the Jewish God spoke not only to the Jewish people but also to the world in the personage of Christ. The Jewish affirmation of the significance and value of history found a yet wider development in Christianity.[27] Hence, any remaining opposition between this world and the world to come cannot deny the world of change. And in that world of change, it is the human being that is considered central. The human is not the Oriental self understood as a portal through which to escape mystically from the world. The human in the here and now is considered as of deep moral and spiritual worth, so that turning away from the human is religiously derelict.

Against Manichaeism and Gnosticism, the Church Fathers emphasized man's central place in creation and the obligation to help people. In this respect, Dawson compares Augustine and Pseudo-Dionysius.[28] Augustine's spiritual ideal was the City of God understood as a force that manifests itself in human society. For the Areopagite the ideal was a speculative mysticism embodied in a system of ritual. Nevertheless, at the thirteenth-century high point of the Church's influence, theocracy was avoided by individuals like St. Francis of Assisi and St. Thomas Aquinas, both of whom acknowledged the reality and value of humanity and the entire order of nature.[29] Aquinas especially broke the old established tradition of Oriental spiritualism and Neo-Platonic idealism.

c. Dawson on modernity. But, like many a synthesis, the medieval synthesis was short-lived. In the face of a certain kind of ossified ritualism—for example, the sale of indulgences and other clerical abuses—the Protestant reformers emphasized the importance of the interior moral order. The Reformation was the revenge of the personalist form of the religious impulse. Dawson sees the Reformation as an attempt to return to something Semitic and nonintellectual.[30] Gone is the Thomistic notion of being, and gone is any hope of reestablishing balance on its basis. Just as reason is irrelevant for one's faith life, so, too, it is irrelevant for God's decrees. Hence, with the future life divinely determined, the reformer makes the most of freedom in the here and now.

In the south of Europe, the medieval synthesis came to wreck on the Renaissance and its resurrection of Hellenic humanist ideals. Dawson is vague on the motivation for this turn, but others[31] locate the motivation in a revulsion at how naked the Middle Ages left the human to deal with such calamities as the Black Death. Remedy for this deficiency was sought in the new sciences. In any case, the common denominator was a turn to the human and the human's perfection in the here and now—secularization. That much of the Christian synthesis lived on.

But the world that the moderns went to meet was the world as approached through the lens of the new sciences. These sciences were remarkably successful in achieving material well-being, though at a cost. The price was a determinist and materialist view of the world that had no place for the person as free and spiritual. Dawson observes that the offered solution was Deism.[32] Since the positive ideas of Deism have no basis in the materialistic world view of modern science, Deism was not an intellectual solution but an outright appeal to elements of the medieval synthesis.

For example, Deism utilizes the Judeo-Christian idea of the creator God. In Deism, however, God exists as the cause of the world conceived in modern scientific terms. In the end, God is subservient to science. Furthermore, God's subservience to modern science eliminated from Deism the supernatural elements of traditional Christianity. Hence, in Deism, the supernaturalism of Christian eschatology is transformed into the idea of the moral perfectibility and the indefinite progress of the human race. But the synthesis of Deism itself was short-lived. The Deist God held no final attraction. The Deist God appeared to be simply a *deus ex machina* who was utilized whenever science met a problem that it could not yet solve. On the contrary, the ideal of progress stirred men's emotions and aroused a genuine religious enthusiasm.

The idea of progress developed in two directions. On the continent,[33] Rousseau used the idea to assume an essential human goodness. That assumption led him to a critical, if not revolutionary attitude toward current exploitative societies. What discredited Rousseau was the Reign of Terror. In England,[34] the breakdown of Deism defaulted to the national and religious character. And so there was no violent break with religion. The moral and social ideals of Puritanism prevailed and channeled the idea of progress into what is known as the industrial revolution. Dawson argues that the real spirit of the industrial age is not to be found in the arid eudaemonism of Mill's utilitarian ethics but in a somber religious asceticism which sacrificed all to the ideals of moral duty and economic power.

Progress and Religion ends with the standard critique of capitalism—its transparently false assumption of ever expanding markets. Dawson interprets Marxism to be fundamentally a movement of spiritual disaffection with the failure of the great movement of material progress to satisfy the instincts of the human element.[35] Two of Dawson's concluding observations are noteworthy. The first is Dawson's reiteration of the critique of urban civilization.[36] Industrialization has produced another case of urbanization. Modern urban civilization no longer has any contact with the soil or with the instinctive life of nature. The entire population lives in a state of nervous tension, even where it has not reached the frenzied activity of American city life. Modern urbanization dries up the "vital reservoir" of human material from which the culturally active elements of the cities, exhausted by the strain of an artificial way of life, can derive new energy. Unable to appreciate this alienation as a frustration of the religious impulse, urban life offers up as a remedy the fleeting technological pleasures of the audio-visual age—just as ancient Rome offered the games of the amphitheatre and the circus. But the religious impulse will not be denied, and so we must wait and see if our age can come to grips with it or whether its frustration will produce more violence.

The second noteworthy thought is Dawson's complaint that the great world religions distract us from the here and now. Concentration on metaphysical conceptions tends to turn our minds away from the material world and practical social activity. Dawson surmises that the religious impulse can be satisfied only in the historical field:

> No religion can entirely dispense with this element. Even in so abstract and metaphysical a faith as that of Buddhism, an intense religious emphasis is attached to the historical personality of the Buddha himself. Nevertheless, in all the oriental religions, as well as in the abstract philosophical religious movements of the West, this element is subordinated to the metaphysical aspect of religion. It is only in Christianity that the historic element acquires such importance that it can be wholly identified with the transcendent and eternal objects of religious faith. The Christian, and he alone, can find a solution to the paradox of the inherence of eternity in time, and of the absolute in the finite which does not empty human life and the material world of their religious significance and value.[37]

To a Thomist, Dawson's narrative of the modern portion of cultural history bespeaks more than the survival of vestiges of the medieval synthesis. Dawson appears to make the modern period a play of sectarian theological ideas rather than the religious impulse of the human intellect. Nevertheless, the implicit workings of the human intellect are playing a role in the historical process. The men of the Enlightenment were more than heirs of a Christian culture. Despite their expressed wishes, they were also intellectors of being. So it is no surprise that they were troubled by the mechanism of modern science. They were correct in thinking themselves to be free and to be harboring a spiritual dimension. Yet the hatred for

Scholasticism and the noncontemplative look of modern science at the world blinded them to the notion of being whose explicit acknowledgment would have explained these ineluctable intimations.

Furthermore, in the wake of an amnesia of the notion of being, it is not surprising that the perfectibility of the human race would catch the interest of the moderns. Like the universe was to the primitives, so too mankind is such a gigantic object that its consideration would force a use of the *ratio entis*. Such a demand could lead one to confuse the goodness of being with the object itself—namely, mankind. But since there is yet no explicit grasp of the human as an intellector of being, as an epiphany of being, we are not yet talking about the good of society mentioned by Aquinas in which the human is the principle part. Hence, unsurprisingly, a commonality between disparate modern social philosophies as liberalism and socialism is that the individual human can be deliberately sacrificed for the good of the whole.

In capitalism the human is sacrificed to the machine; in Marxism the human is sacrificed to the glorious future of communism. Only an understanding of the human as an intellector of being can place the brakes on these modern ideologies—though, as Dawson has noted and as a Thomist would agree, modernism seems to have conspired, through urbanization, to camouflage the insight.[38] The Thomist knows what work is assigned. Somehow the Thomist must reawaken a sense of the dignity of each human. Along with brothers and sisters in a common faith, the Thomist will strive to do this by rekindling in the minds of people the intuition of being while the others do the same through offering the revelation of God through Jesus Christ. Both can be hopeful because the human is already an intellector of being long before the human realizes it. If properly crafted, the words of the Thomist will not fall on deaf ears. Nor will the words of the believer necessarily suffer that fate. The human, as an intellector of being, is eerily congruent with the Christian revelation. Dawson points out that many in the world once realized that congruity, and Christianity flourished. It can happen again.

5. Tracey Rowland's "Augustinian Thomism"

By commenting upon Christopher Dawson's reflections about religion as a basis for culture, I have tried to illustrate how the Thomistic psychology of the intellector of being is operative in all the vagaries of cultural history. This thesis means that philosophy trumps economics and sociology as the hermeneutical tool for understanding culture. Philosophy is the bedrock of all societies, and a practitioner of Thomistic philosophy is in a position to appreciate the different authentic cultural responses to that philosophy and to correct aberrations.

If I understand her, Tracey Rowland, in her engaging *Culture and the Thomist Tradition after Vatican II*, does not see it that way. Heavily indebted to philosopher Alasdair MacIntyre and theologian David Schindler, Rowland views modernity, especially in the Anglo-liberal tradition, as a culture impervious to the Christian message. The people that inhabit that world have been formed in a culture whose values make it impossible to appreciate the words of the Church. Obstacles in modernity include these: fostering decision making by reference to bureaucratic norms, marginalizing the transcendence of beauty, engendering an anti-historical "culture of forgetting," and prioritizing economic performance and "humanist" projects that incline even denominational loyalists to a constructive atheism.[39] Again, in her judgment, modernity cannot be a *praeparatio evangelii.*

This us–against–them stance is related to the thesis that rationality is tradition-dependent. I understand this thesis to mean that tradition does not simply direct or hold our attention to something that we would have missed in our distraction but that tradition performs a constitutive role in the appearance of rational norms. Hence, language that has one sense in a tradition or culture has a different sense in another tradition. Rowland accuses those at Vatican II of a naivety in their believing that the Church could flourish and prosper in the modern world. She rests the reason for the naivety squarely at the feet of the Thomists at Vatican II. Their Thomism was too rational, and so they were blind to the power of culture to form human character in ways inimical to the Christian message.[40] This problem persists through John Paul II's *Fides et Ratio* (1998). The Pope fails to realize that his implicit philosophy of noncontradiction, finality, causality, and the concept of the person as free and intelligent involve the assumption of an ordered universe. Immersion within another cultural world undermines the ability of plain persons to reach an understanding of this implicit philosophy.[41] Thomists must finally realize that, not the halls of academe, but the realm of culture is the site of the battle of the *Logos.*

Rowland enjoins her fellow Thomists to take more account of the formative role of culture in the thought of people and to replace a rationalistic disembodied approach with one that accords a greater role to nonrational factors. Rejecting the idea of the autonomy of culture from theology and thus echoing Augustine's "Unless you believe you shall not understand," Rowland labels herself an Augustinian Thomist.[42] Relying upon MacIntyre, she concedes to reason a preparatory role in conversion. Dialectical analysis is important for uncovering the inadequacies of positions opposed to Catholicism. But following dialectical analysis is sociology—an experience with the wealth of the Christian tradition as doing a better job in the task of formation of the self.[43]

Despite an agreement that current Western culture constitutes a huge problem for evangelization and that Rowland does a fine analytic job of sketching the issues, I believe that a chasm exists between the theses of my monograph and those of hers. The point of contention is not whether Thomism has a philosophy of culture. Like Rowland, I have tried to show that it does. Rather, our difference stems from the role of rationality vis-à-vis culture. Is rationality tradition-dependent or is rationality tradition-initiating? From one's answer follows one's stance to culture—even the current Western one. I have labored to show that the human is not so victim to nonrational factors that the light of reason is snuffed out. Despite ourselves, we are intellectors of being. Even in the most ordinary person, conscious outcroppings of this intellection exist. Hence, if the Thomist is sufficiently clever, the Thomist can discern these effects and can utilize them to lead people to an appreciation of this pregnant philosophical truth.

My understanding of Thomistic psychology places the Christian or any proponent of Thomism in an engaged relation to culture. No culture will be viewed as impervious to the Christian message because, at bottom, every person has a Thomist intellect that cannot be denied. This intellect, ineradicably stamped with the notion of being, disposes (no matter how remotely) the culture to—and creates an openness for—the Christian message. No culture will trump Thomistic psychology. The Thomist is confirmed in a dialogical relation with others. Simultaneously, the same psychology will alert the Thomist to the problems that the dialogue can encounter. The data of sense can camouflage the spontaneous intellection of being, and the use of being to contemplate grandiose objects can lead to investing the object with a quasi-divine status that occludes true epiphanies of being in the Creator and the human person. These pitfalls have many permutations. It will take much patient listening to diagnose the culture correctly in order to understand how to begin talking with it.

In contrast, the implication of Rowland's viewpoint seems to be a fortress or ghetto Catholicism that writes off dialogue with modern culture because of its antithetical attitudes to Christianity. Rowland says, "The Augustinian Thomist position proposed in this work is very much in accord with the judgment of Origen that it is better to die in the desert than to end up in the service of the Egyptians, or one might add, end up in a position where the 'Chosen People' start to believe that they *are Egyptians* because all cultural traces of their specific differences have been suppressed."[44]

6. Alasdair MacIntyre and the Notion of Truth

So who is correct? First, I do not believe that the above intellection of being version of Aquinas can, like many Enlightenment philosophies, be deconstructed and be shown to rest on nonrational assumptions.[45] For example, as the analyses of chapters II and III indicate, none of this work by the Thomist would involve assuming an ordered universe, as Rowland insists. Frankly, it is embarrassing how minimal is the requisite data to initiate Aquinas' line of thought. However, the minimalism of the data is what assures the presence of the data in any cultural setting. What is utilized is an epistemology of abstraction. There, the "assumption" is the reality of the data of sense in which one intellects the notion of being. This sense realism presumes only a rudimentary ability to be informed by the other. The required data of sense do not have to be full-blooded substances or more exotic things that only a participant in a particular culture could recognize. Rather, the panoply of real colors, shapes, surfaces, and motions are sufficiently general to be incontestable. For example, perhaps we do not know who perceives the exact shade, but everyone sees color; perhaps we do not know who sees the exact configuration, but everyone sees shape; perhaps we do not know the exact subject of the motion, but everyone knows that something is moving. These undeniable real data suffice to intellect an analogical notion of being since the reality of each item is not apart from their differences. One cannot understand the reality of the item without including in that understanding the differences.

Furthermore, I explained that Aquinas exploits the intellectual insight of being in the data of sensation to undergird the subsequent elements of the "implicit philosophy" of *Fides et Ratio*—namely, noncontradiction, causality, and the freedom and value of the human person.[46] Below I will note that MacIntyre's "philosophical imagination" acknowledges the ability to be informed by the other. Yet, as practiced upon reality given in sensation, this ability, for MacIntyre, apparently finds nothing of philosophical significance.[47] In sum, as I explained in chapter V, it is the Thomist who can out-narrate the hedonist, the utilitarian, the Kantian, the Rawlsian, and the Heideggerian.

Second, to deal with the appearance of historical and cultural relativism in her tradition-dependent rationality, Rowland enlists the aid of Alasdair MacIntyre. In his 1994 article, "Moral Relativism, Truth and Justification," edited in a Festschrift for Peter Geach and Elizabeth Anscombe, MacIntyre witnesses his commitment to Aquinas' understanding of truth: "When and insofar as, on Aquinas's type of account, a particular person's intellect is adequate to some particular subject-matter with which it is engaged in its thinking, it is what the objects of that thinking in fact are which makes it the case that that person's thoughts about those objects are what they are—and, in respect of the content of that thought, nothing else."[48]

But what truth is is one thing, knowing that truth exists is something else. How do we become aware of truth? MacIntyre goes on to describe the discernment of truth in the ethical area. He argues that, though ethical ideas are viewpoint-dependent, good reasons exist for adopting one over another. When a rival viewpoint explains the intractable problems of another viewpoint as well as problems of its own, then one has "excellent reasons" for accepting it as true.[49] Usually, explanatory success is not considered a guarantor of truth. The ball-and-stick model of the molecule is a very successful explanatory model, but no one thinks that it is literally true. But behind this critique of relativism is a position on truth.

Earlier in the article, McIntyre interprets the medieval truth formula, *adequatio rei et intellectus*, as an adequation of the intellect to an end.[50] This interpretation turns the defense of realism away from Dummett's charge of a "conceptual leap" to "some state of affairs obtaining independently of our knowledge" in order to satisfy an asserted sentence. Rather, now truth is the prior notion and justifiability is secondary. In other words, because the intellect has already conformed itself to some end, issues of justifiability can follow. MacIntyre describes the intellect's end of truth as a viewpoint that does not "suffer from limitations, partialities and one-sidedness of a merely local point of view."[51]

In a 2001 article, "Truth as a Good: A Reflection on *Fides et Ratio*," and as the title indicates, MacIntyre continues his interpretation of the truth formula. The encyclical presents a realist understanding of truth, and amid current analytic discussions of truth—such as prosentential theory (Grover, Camp, and Belknap) and two forms of correspondence theory[52]—MacIntyre defends his understanding of realism. Truth is fundamentally had when our judgments are placed in relation to the order of the whole: "It is from the relationship of particular truths to 'the truth' that the goodness of particular truths is in part derived."[53]

Likewise, and contra Crispin Wright, the question of warrant is different from that of truth. Truth implies how things are *sub specie Dei*.[54] That possibility makes sense of the directed movement of our inquiries towards an ultimate end. So, as MacIntyre sees it, Aquinas' notion of truth is an intensely personal affair. Here MacIntyre makes some brief references to the *De Veritate*. For Aquinas, every human being has by nature a desire for happiness achieved only in union with God, recognized as the truth from which all truth flows.[55] "Detached" from this larger teleological setting, Aquinas' theory of truth will be ineffectual.

On the contrary, if "attached," Aquinas' theory of truth will be ineffectual. MacIntyre's understanding of truth in Aquinas has unmistakable echoes of Transcendental Thomism. For Transcendental Thomism also, truth is apportioned to our judgments insofar as our judgments fit into the mind's innate dynamism to an infinite term.[56] Yet serious philosophical and textual problems exist in "attaching" Aquinas' account of truth to this larger teleological setting. All Thomists agree that the mind is fundamentally inclined to the truth. The issue is whether this inclination should be basically understood in terms of an inclination to receive or an inclination to project. Transcendental Thomists opt for the latter.

The "truth" of the term of intellectual dynamism is established by a procedure called *retorsion* or *performative contradiction*. Transcendental Thomists consider retorsion to be identical with Aristotle's defense of the principle of noncontradiction in the fourth book of the *Metaphysics*.[57] Retorsion vindicates the objectivity of an item by displaying the item's ineluctability or unrestrictedness. In other words, doubt about a perspective makes sense because we can think apart from the perspective. For example, I can doubt what I am seeing through a camera lens because I know that I can remove the camera and see the object with my eyes. But if a perspective is unrestricted or ineluctable, the thought of the object as outside the perspective is nugatory, so any reason for doubting it is supposedly removed. In his mentioned equation of truth with nonpartial perspectives, MacIntyre appears to be following the retorsion methodology to validate his confidence that the end of our intellect is truth.

But the retorsion methodology can be easily deconstructed or outnarrated. The case for possible distortion or untruth does not rest simply on a perceived restrictedness to the perspective but also upon a familiarity with less encompassing perspectives. It is not by a look ahead but by a look back that one deconstructs retorsion. The look back to more restricted perspectives acquaints one with the ideas of something standing outside a perspective and with the perspective placing the thing in a different light. Perspectives can be limited and distortive. One naturally and correctly wonders if such is the case with an unrestricted perspective. Unrestrictedness is, then, indecisive as an indicator of truth. The unrestrictedness of a perspective could quite well follow simply from the fundamentality of the perspective. In other words, an unlimited viewpoint may still be a limited one, but it appears as unlimited because it is so fundamental.

Hence, because other limited but fundamental viewpoints may exist, relativism would seem to be still in play. For all we know, all of us may be headed to absurdity rather than to truth.[58] Hence, that one position is less partial because it explains the problems of another as well as its own is not "an excellent reason" for the position's truth. MacIntyre's critique of ethical relativism presupposes a theory of truth that is itself questionable. What is needed here is an intellectual insight into real items that provide the ineluctable perspective. Since the perspective is discovered or drawn from the real, then one is confident that the perspective is objective and true. I have argued that such is the notion of being. MacIntyre does seem to admit an a posteriori capacity possessed by the human mind. In "Moral Relativism," he speaks of the "philosophical and moral imagination" which enables one to "learn" another moral standpoint and to see one's original standpoint from that view.[59] Such a mental capacity, in my opinion, is at odds with tradition-dependent rationality because it implies that rationality is tradition-neutral. But be that as it may, is it not arbitrary to restrict learning just to other "perspectives?" Besides another perspective, why cannot reality be one of the things about which we can learn?

7. David Schindler and *Communio Personarum*

As I mentioned, along with McIntyre, another intellectual confrere of Rowland is David Schindler. At the end of *Culture and the Thomist Tradition*, Rowland provides extensive bibliographies of both men. In my opinion, as engaging and knowledgeable as Rowland is, Schindler is the more profound thinker. Unfortunately, Rowland does not fully present the scope of Schindler's thought. In that wider perspective, many agreements exist between myself and Schindler, though fundamental disagreements persist. I would like to conclude my discussion of Rowland with a discussion of Schindler.

In respect to the Western liberal state, Schindler sees a problem similar to one I found with Rawls. I said that, as a noncomprehensive doctrine, political liberalism created (at the least) a sociological drift away from any comprehensive doctrine. Once one realizes this trap, it is doubtful that any party in the original position would sign on to the principles of justice. Schindler expresses this sociological drift this way: "[The political legal institutions of liberal states] tend . . . to act as referees whose purpose is solely to keep the societal playing field level, by insuring the equal freedom of all individual citizens to choose and to protect their rights. What this implies is that such political-legal institutions tend always to act in favor of the (*empty*) *form* of freedom and never in favor of the (*substantive*) *ideology* of any person or group in society. Hence, we get 'proceduralism': 'form' as a matter of principle displaces 'substance' in society's official-legal workings."[60]

Schindler observes that, far from being neutral, the liberal state, by its proclaimed neutrality, is actually Cartesian. Just as Descartes viewed body and mind in and through clear and distinct ideas, so too, the liberal state views itself vis-à-vis any comprehensive doctrine. Hence, Schindler observes that the only way to begin—without begging the question—is by asking not "*whether* the state should actualize someone's 'confession,' but *which* 'confession' it will actualize, and in what ways."[61]

Schindler is unabashedly Catholic in his answer to that question. Following John Paul II's proclamation of evangelization, Schindler proposes a view of the state informed by *Gaudium et Spes*, para. 22, in which Christ is the source for all thinking about the human being. As the Council's document states: Christ "in the very revelation of the mystery of the Father and of his love, fully reveals man to himself and brings to light his most high calling." Hence, prior to moral, economic, and political affairs, every human person is defined by a capacity for God. Second, deepening the relation to God in Christ is necessary for deepening the integrity of nature. Third, concrete human nature's path to integrity is the mysteries of faith entailed in Christ's revelation—that is, Trinitarian love through the Marian and sacramental Church. Fourth, all humans are called to holiness. Fifth, as transformed by the *One who is sent*, each Christian is called to a missionary task. Schindler regards America as what John Paul calls an intermediate situation of entire groups of baptized without a living sense of the faith. They desperately search for meaning and inner life but sink deeper into consumerism and materialism. Such a situation is ripe for a Christo-centric re-evangelization.

As sectarian as the above thinking sounds, Schindler cleverly argues that it perfectly accommodates respect for consciences: "Given the pope's terms, the primary emphasis is placed rather on seeking to infuse the state with a primarily non-coercive 'confession.'"[62] Because of each person's constitutive relation to God, our relations to each other should be marked with respect and love. Hence, the Gospel should always be proposed and never imposed.

Fully admitting my inability to do justice to the richness of Schindler's theological narrative, in his own theological way, Schindler supports my thesis that substantive truth is compatible with tolerance. Hence, even unbelievers would want to live, not in a neutral state, but in a Christian confessional state. The strategy, if not the theology, is central to my monograph. But Schindler does more than theologize. The philosopher is also able to elaborate the intrinsic and constitutive relation of humans to God. He remarks, "I am not at all implying here that human nature itself does not already indicate the path to be followed in realizing its own integrity, or that human nature's imaging of God is not inscribed already in the spiritual powers that distinguish the human creature from all other creatures."[63] To discover how Schindler understands this imaging, one must turn to another published article.

In "God and the End of Intelligence: Knowledge as Relationship," while giving an exegesis of *Fides et Ratio*, Schindler insists that "the formal object of theology already 'contains' the formal object of philosophy, and thus (in the one historical order) is already 'inside' the formal object of philosophy, by way of a kind of 'anticipation.'"[64] To explain the claim, he turns to Henri de Lubac's interpretation of a text of Aquinas. In his *De Veritate* XXII, 2, Aquinas asserts an implicit knowledge of God in all that we know and in all that we love. Schindler correctly notes that the assertion presupposes a context set by the doctrine of creation. Hence, the meaning of the assertion is this: "All knowers know God implicitly in all that they know, because every object of knowledge is a creature, and because, as a creature, it bears within it the likeness of the Creator."

Schindler immediately proceeds to de Lubac's interpretation as set out in his *The Discovery of God*. For de Lubac, *De Veritate* XXII, 2 expresses an ontology of knowledge in which the human intellect is a priori orientated to the Infinite and in which this a priori orientation is used constitutively in our consciousness of finite objects.[65] Strictly speaking, then, we do not prove God's existence, for God is already asserted in any finite item as finite—for example, in a concept or in a premise.

In his own elaboration of this ontology of knowledge, Schindler makes many claims significant for his own vision. The claim from which the others flow is this: "Both the subject and object of knowledge are from the beginning grasped implicitly in terms of an (asymmetrically) ordered *movement from and toward* God; both are grasped (implicitly) *from 'inside'* *relation* to God; both are grasped (implicitly) thereby *in their unity* as *gifts* from God."[66]

He also writes (on page 528), "Knowledge is first and foremost a matter of relation." Schindler offers a schematic list suggestive of implications of this assertion.[67] First, knowledge is "indwelling." Here, Schindler borrows from Polanyi, who claimed that to rely on a theory for understanding nature is to interiorize the theory into the data. Second, in light of de Lubac's thought that we require the Infinite in order to profile or objectify the finite, Schindler recasts the principle of identity. He says that "the identity of things is never first a mechanical identity, as though the identity of anything is given apart from relation." Third, our knowledge is both with and without foundations. Knowledge is the former because the constitutive relation to the Infinite reveals things for what they are; knowledge is the latter because seeing things for what they are requires the constitutive relation. Again, the constitutive relation is the hidden dimension for the maxim that truth is *adequatio intellectus et rei* in which *rei* is some finite thing. Fourth, from the above gloss of the identity principle, it follows that the relation of any entity to another is never simply additive in nature. Rather, "the identity of each is always and from the beginning structured with an intrinsic openness to the O(o)ther(s)." Though Schindler does not bring it up, the fourth implication would seem to be the basis for how the person is vulnerable to cultural and social influences. Hence, our basic relational character to the Infinite can be camouflaged or in some sense superseded by relations antithetical to our basic one. Consequently, Rowland can speak of the importance of culture's formative influence. Fifth, analysis should be reconceived organismically rather than mechanistically. In other words, analysis perceives not simply parts but parts precisely *of wholes*. Analysis should not fool us into thinking that the whole is not prior. Sixth, the copula does more than function as a connective. It has an existential and enriching sense in which its role is to place the subject in relation to the whole of what is, to the Infinite. Finally, seventh, the modern dualism of subject and object is overcome. For both are given in the more primordial unity of the self's constitutive and asymmetrical relation to God.

Schindler is such a veteran systematic thinker that he touches upon all the major issues, so it is difficult to know where to begin. But obviously his central point for philosophers reflecting upon person and culture is his ontology of knowledge. So I would like to restrict myself to comments on that thesis. First, given its centrality for Schindler and given Rowland's indebtedness to Schindler, it is remarkable that the epistemology of cognitional dynamism to the Infinite never surfaces in Rowland's *Culture and the Thomist Tradition.* As primordially characterizing all humans, the epistemology would belie Rowland's thesis of tradition-dependent rationality. Hence, no one should be so quick to write off dialogue with another tradition, as Rowland dismisses dialogue with the Western liberal tradition. For despite the formation of minds by a culture, the forces of that culture cannot supplant an immediate relation of minds to the creator. From the perspective of this constitutive epistemology, no culture should produce ideas totally unrelated to God. As object of intellectual dynamism, God will "indwell" all cognitional contents. Hence, contra Rowland, a dialogical approach to non-Christian cultures that is "genetic" seems apropos. Like my psychology of the intellector of being, the epistemology of intellectual dynamism demands from its proponents, not dismissiveness, but tolerant dialogical behavior with all.

Second, how effective is Schindler's ontology of knowledge? As a piece of philosophy, not very.[68] Perhaps in Schindler's summary of de Lubac, the reader has already heard echoes of my last section's summary of Transcendental Thomism. Such a hearing would be correct. Any question about de Lubac's close affiliation with Transcendental Thomism is dispelled by his *The Discovery of God.* Chapters 2 and 3 are laced with Transcendental Thomist themes. In fact, de Lubac approvingly quotes from Maréchal's *Le Point de départ de la métaphysique.* These quotes are unabashed expressions of Maréchal's Kantian transcendental philosophy. Concerning these quotes, de Lubac says that they "sum up and provide the foundation"[69] for his chapters 2 and 3. But this liaison of de Lubac with Maréchal only transports my earlier stated problems with Transcendental Thomism to Schindler. In sum, *pace* retorsion or performative self-contradiction, you never really know that the dynamism of the intellect expresses more than a quirk of the mind. Hence, Schindler goes question begging to claim that the dynamism is a gift from God and reveals the world for what it is. A philosopher can well wonder if the dynamism is objective and if it provides objective knowledge of things in turn.[70]

The intellector of being approach does not suffer this skepticism. Being is not a constitutive *proiectum* but an *abstractum* taken from sensed items that are self-manifestly real. A phenomenology of sensation shows no need for something a priori to render the data real nor something like an image or a memory to mediate the presence of the data. The data announce themselves as real. Moreover, the same phenomenology shows that the appreciation of the real data as finite is not properly basic but subsequent to juxtaposing the data to the *abstractum* of being.[71]

But by referencing de Lubac's citation of Aquinas' *De Veritate* XXII, 2, does not Schindler have Aquinas on his side? I am quite familiar with this text and many others used to underwrite the Transcendental Thomist interpretation of Aquinas' philosophy of knowledge. My a posteriori accounts of these texts have been published in many formats and I will not repeat the accounts here.[72] Instead I want to finish my discussion of Schindler with another important topic raised by his interpretation of *De Veritate* XXII, 2. A discussion of the topic requires a theological aside, however.

Schindler's account admitted that "the doctrine of creation" is the context for his interpretation. As noted, this doctrine had already been elucidated by the Christo-centric *Gaudium et Spes*. In other words, by the revelation of Christ, we learn why we were created, namely, to share in the intimate life of God. Now Schindler assumes that a creature with that destiny must be created with the ontology of knowledge that he describes. Is that assumption correct? As a fellow believer, I agree that God has called us to Himself. This divine call cannot be without effect. But the question is whether a called human nature must be a Lubacian human nature. Must God's call effect a human nature with an a priori and cognitionally constitutive dynamism to the Infinite? Schindler thinks so, I believe, because the alternative is the pure and closed nature position of Cajetan so justly criticized by de Lubac for its extrinsicism to grace. Cajetan makes happiness that we can achieve without grace to be so integral and complete that the offer of a supernatural divine life appears as irrelevant to human nature. But I believe that Schindler overlooks a tertium quid for understanding called human nature. That third alternative is what I have been calling the intellector of being. I wish to summarize some previously published material on the nature/grace distinction.[73]

If the reader recalls my above interpretation in chapter III of Aquinas' natural knowledge of God, then the reader will remember my claim that one cannot be an intellector of being without grasping its causal implications. Hence, I mentioned how Aquinas could integrate Leibniz's question reiterated by Heidegger—"Why is there something rather than nothing?" Also, because Aquinas' first cause instantiates being, then, mutatis mutandis, our analogical knowledge of being is some analogical knowledge of God.[74] This employment of analogy, understood as the grasp of "sameness in difference," delivers a human nature oriented to God with profound interest yet without any shadow of exigency. How does our knowledge of the creator by means of analogical being perform this balancing act?

The trick lies in the dual character of the analogical commonality, or analogon; analogons are known and unknown, visible yet hidden. Because we intellectually see the sameness through the differences of the instances, we see the sameness imperfectly and confusedly. The intellection of analogons is both a success and a failure. Hence, there is both joy and yearning. Insofar as we intellect the sameness, there is success and delight. It is not merely hyperbole that leads Aquinas, at *Summa Contra Gentiles* I, 5, to agree with Aristotle that the little we know of higher substances is loved and desired more than all our knowledge about less noble substances. Furthermore, this little and imperfect knowledge produces "intense joy" (*vehemens sit gaudium eius*) and brings the "greatest perfection to the soul" (*maximam perfectionem animae*). Yet insofar as the intellection of the sameness occurs through the differences of the instances, or analogates, the analogon is veiled, so there is disappointment.

Consequently, once we have some sense that being is the nature of the creator, we understand our analogical knowledge of being to be some grasp of the creator. Our peering into being is now understood as peering into more than an abstraction. Such a reorientation produces an exquisite satisfaction. Yet, since the vision is analogical, there is frustration and an exquisite yearning. How can a mind informed as such by reality—and thus in possession of a natural excellence—not also be profoundly interested in knowing if the creator will supersede this analogical presence by an actual introduction to the created mind? The Church's revelation of Christ cannot but have the greatest interest for and attention of the intellector of being, for whom the following would be a burning question: "Could the creator have actually communicated to humans in human history in the personage of Jesus Christ?"

The Thomistic understanding of the human, at the achievement of its natural powers abstracting from grace, is that of an analogical intellector of being. As gratuitous as grace remains, grace stays genuinely relevant for such a knower. Aquinas' a posteriori ontology of knowledge can provide what today's theologian wants from philosophy, but without the disastrous epistemological liabilities of Transcendental Thomism.

8. Conclusion

I have tried to show how Aquinas' natural law ethics, as it ties into Aquinas' deep psychology of the intellector of being, is a fount for cultural identity. The call of Aquinas' ethics for respect and solicitude for one's fellows cannot but generate different cultural forms. Just as living the moral life will do something different for you than for me, so too, the moral life will differentiate societies. Here it is important to remember that natural law means more than just prohibitions, though the word *law* tends to keep negative norms at the front of our minds. In Aquinas' natural law ethics, murder, adultery, theft, lying, and the like will never be morally good. But when all these negative norms are observed, the obligation to be respectful and solicitous of persons remains.

And who can say how this respect and solicitude will be realized? For example, those who were born in the 1920s could never have imagined that for some of them the moral life would take the form of naval fliers and marines in the far-flung reaches of the Pacific Ocean. Such are the resources for identity of Aquinas' ethics because behind the good stands the notion of being and the resources of analogy, or sameness-in-difference. It is not surprising that you find the same resources for identity in the parade of saints in a religion whose greatest theologians said that God was Being Itself.

Grounded in its own philosophical analyses, Aquinas' thinking receives a boost in the anthropological studies of Dawson. What I have called the intellection of being and the implications thereof can be integrated with what Dawson calls the religious impulse and intuition. Hence, one can read Dawson's monumental narrative of cultural history as illustrating the cultural vicissitudes of the human person understood as an intellector of being. Such integration not only provides a striking concrete portrayal of Aquinas' ideas, further cementing their truth, but also generates a different attitude toward other cultures than is found in Tracey Rowland.

To repeat what I said at the end of chapter III, enough material exists to know that the notion of being controls, and has always controlled, human psychology. In the light of this psychology, the Thomist goes out to meet others. The Thomist realizes that thick walls of cultures or philosophies will be found. But the walls will not be impenetrable. Aquinas' psychology provides a commensurating discourse. Being cannot be eliminated from the heart of the human.

Notes:

[1] Vytis Čiubrinskas, "Identity and the Revival of Tradition in Lithuania: an Insider's View," *Folk* 42 (2000): 26.

[2] Ibid., 39–40.

[3] Benedict Anderson, *Imagined Communities: Reflections on the Origin and Spread of Nationalism* (Verso: London, 1991). In his "Between Soup and Soap: Iconic Nationality, Mass Media and Pop Culture in Contemporary Lithuania," *Lituanus* 46 (2000): 16, Arturas Tereškinas echoes views similar to Čiubrinskas' and also notes an indebtedness to Anderson. For a reflective survey of various philosophies of culture since the eighteenth century from the perspective of the Transcendental Thomist philosophy of being, see Louis Dupré, *Metaphysics and Culture* (Milwaukee: Marquette University Press, 1994). For some comments on Transcendental Thomist methodology, see my section 6 in this chapter, "Alasdair MacIntyre and the Notion of Truth."

[4] In my opinion, Anderson's analysis runs afoul of the fact that the nineteenth-century Lithuanian national revival was driven by Lithuanian peasants who wanted to be Catholic and not Russian Orthodox but also no longer the serfs of the Polish or Polonized gentry and landlords. Their solution was to be Catholic and Lithuanian.

[5] Consider this remark on Albert Schweitzer's thoughts on the basis of culture: "[Schweitzer's] 'stress on life' remains lacking in substantial metaphysical grounding as well as in rigor of conception. Nonetheless, his recognition that culture can die and that the ethical attitude is basic to vitalizing and enriching culture is very important for understanding the nature of culture." Atherton Lowery, "The Metaphysics of Culture: Its Being, Its Life, and Its Death," *Proceedings of the American Catholic Philosophical Association* 77 (2003): 255.

[6] Richard Rorty, "The Priority of Democracy to Philosophy" in *Objectivity, Relativism, and Truth* (Cambridge: Cambridge University Press, 1991), 175–196. In his "Faith, Culture, and Reason: Analogous Language and Truth," *Proceedings of the American Catholic Philosophical Association* 77 (2003), David B. Burrell conflates "inquiry" with explicit philosophy: "In short, 'relativism' gives way to the human fact that all inquiry takes place within a tradition, and the specter which it evoked turns out to be the residual shadow of our faith in 'pure reason,' that is, in the pretension of human inquiry bereft of any tradition. So the discovery (on the part of reason) that every inquiry employs presuppositions which cannot themselves be rationally justified opens the way to self-knowledge on the part of enlightenment philosophy itself, which can then take its place among the traditions" (p. 4). As I will explain, the implicit philosophy of the intellection of being is what initiates traditions with their explicit philosophies.

[7] Ibid., 181.

[8] Consider this: "It is true, as I have already observed, that in primitive religion it is the sense of external cosmic transcendence which predominates. Nevertheless this cannot be entirely detached from the internal intuition of transcendence even though the latter is obscure, confused and rudimentary." Christopher Dawson, *Religion and Culture* (New York: Sheed & Ward: 1948), 39.

[9] Christopher Dawson, *Progress and Religion: An Historical Enquiry* (Washington, DC: The Catholic University of America Press, 2001).

[10] Ibid., 52.

[11] Ibid., 69.

[12] "The dynamic element in primitive culture is to be found rather in the sphere of direct religious experience than in that of conscious rational enquiry. It may seem paradoxical to suggest that the starting point of human progress is to be found in the highest type of knowledge—the intuition of pure being, but it must be remembered that intellectually, at least, man's development is not so much from the lower to the higher as from the confused to the distinct." Ibid., 76–77.

[13] Cf., "Rather, our species has—ever since it developed language—been making up a nature for itself. This nature has been developed through ever larger, richer, more muddled, and more painful syntheses of opposing values." Richard Rorty, "Cosmopolitanism with Emancipation," in *Objectivity, Relativity, and Truth,* 213.

[14] "The primitive has the same ultimate experience of reality on the deeper level of consciousness as the civilized man, but he has no criterion to separate what is spiritually transcendent from what is naturally extraordinary. He cannot connect his intuition of transcendent power with any rational metaphysical system; but he can superimpose upon it some image or intuition of external reality which makes a powerful psychological appeal to him, since primitive thought develops by association and images rather than by arguments and ideas." Christopher Dawson, *Religion and Culture,* 40.

[15] Dawson, *Progress and Religion,* 91.

[16] Ibid., 94.

[17] Ibid., 95.

[18] Ibid., 58–62. Also, pp. 164–165.

[19] Josef Pieper, *Leisure: The Basis of Culture* (New York: The New American Library of World Literature, 1963), 102–103.

[20] Dawson, *Religion and Progress,* 99.

[21] Ibid., 105.

[22] Though my application is different, my strategy is similar to Jacques Maritain's in "The Natural Mystical Experience and the Void," in his *Ransoming the Time* (New York: Gordian Press, 1972). For Maritain (pp. 279–280, n. 18), the Indian mystic attains God by a heightened experience of the *esse* of the mystic's own soul.

[23] Dawson, *Progress and Religion,* 106.

[24] Ibid., 109–110.

[25] Ibid., 112–119.

[26] Ibid., 120–124.

[27] Ibid., 125.

[28] Ibid., 131.

[29] Ibid., 135–137.

[30] Ibid., 142.

[31] Jacques Maritain, *Integral Humanism: Temporal and Spiritual Problems of a New Christendom* (Notre Dame, IN: University of Notre Dame Press, 1973), 15.

[32] Dawson, *Progress and Religion,* 148–149.

[33] Ibid., 150–157.

[34] Ibid., 158–160.

[35] Ibid., 163.

[36] Ibid., 164–165

[37] Ibid., 188–189.

[38] Cf., "This means that the naturalized Hegelian analogue of 'intrinsic human dignity' is the comparative dignity of a group with which a person identifies herself. Nations or churches or movements are, on this view, shining historical examples not because they re-

flect rays emanating from a higher source, but because of contrast-effects—comparisons with other, worse communities. Persons have dignity not as an interior luminescence, but because they share in such contrast-effects." Richard Rorty, "Postmodernist Bourgeois Liberalism" in *Objectivity, Relativism, and Truth*, 200.

[39] Tracey Rowland, *Culture and the Thomist Tradition after Vatican II* (London: Routledge, 2003), 160–161.

[40] An exception might well be the Lithuania inter-war Thomist, Stasys Šalkauskis. See my "Thomistic Reflections on Stasys Šalkauskis' Philosophy of Culture," *Soter* (Journal of the Faculty of Theology, Vytautas Magnus University, Kaunas, Lithuania) 29 (2009): 7–16.

[41] Tracey Rowland, *Culture and the Thomist Tradition after Vatican II*, 130.

[42] Ibid., 100.

[43] Ibid., 131

[44] Ibid., p. 165. The following author appears to acknowledge a metaphysical commensurating factor while acknowledging that cultural attempts to realize metaphysical truth will always take the form of analogates, not the analogon itself: "Why are all cultures, on the one hand, just particular cultures and, thus, differentiated one from another, and why are they at the same time open toward each other, capable of mutually purifying each other and of merging with each other? There are also, of course, positivistic answers, and I do not want to go into them here. It seems to me that at this point in particular one cannot avoid reference to the metaphysical dimension. A meeting of cultures is possible because man, in all the variety of his history and of his social structures and customs, is a single being, one and the same. This one being, man, is however touched and affected in the very depth of his existence by truth itself. The fundamental openness of all men to others, and the agreement in essentials to be found even between those cultures farthest removed from each other, can only be explained by the hidden way our souls have been touched by truth. But the variety, which can even lead to a closed attitude, comes in the first instance from the limitation of the human mind: no one can grasp the whole of anything, but many and varied perceptions and forms come together in a sort of mosaic, suggested by the way that each is complementary with regard to the others: in order to form the whole, each needs all the others. Only in the interrelating of all great works of culture can man approach the unity and wholeness of his true nature." Joseph Cardinal Ratzinger, *Truth and Tolerance: Christian Belief and World Religions*, trans. by Henry Taylor (San Francisco: Ignatius Press, 2003), 64–65.

[45] Ibid., 129.

[46] Also contra MacIntyre, mentioned by Rowland on p. 86, this Thomist concept of human nature is elaborated without any intrinsic reference to the concepts of grace, creation, and providence. On the openness of the said nature to the order of grace, see my *Being and Some Twentieth-Century Thomists* (New York: Fordham University Press, 2003), 294–306.

[47] Despite Aquinas' mantra-like claim that all our knowledge takes its origin from sensible things, Alasdair MacIntyre, while claiming to express Aquinas, contends that "there is no way of identifying, characterizing, or classifying that particular datum in a way relevant to the purposes of theoretical inquiry except in terms of some prior theoretical or doctrinal commitment," *Three Rival Versions of Moral Enquiry* (Notre Dame, IN: University of Notre Dame Press, 1990), 17; also 111–112, on the data as "too meager and [they] underdetermine any characterization at the required level." Likewise, in his *First Principles, Final Ends, and Contemporary Philosophical Issues* (Milwaukee: Marquette University Press, 1990), 8–9, MacIntyre enjoins Thomists to accept "antifoundational arguments."

⁴⁸ Reedited by Kelvin Knight in *The MacIntyre Reader* (Notre Dame, IN: University of Notre Dame Press, 1998), 214.

⁴⁹ Ibid., 219.

⁵⁰ Ibid., 207.

⁵¹ Ibid., 208. Cf., "The objectivity of human knowing, then, rests upon an unrestricted intention and an unconditioned result. Because the intention is unrestricted, it is not restricted to the immanent content of knowing . . . ." Bernard J. F. Lonergan, "Cognitional Structure," in F. E. Crowe, *Collection: Papers by Bernard Lonergan, S.J.* (New York: Herder and Herder, 1967), 230.

⁵² Alasdair MacIntyre, "Truth as a Good: A Reflection on *Fides et Ratio*," ed. by James McEvoy and Michael Dunne, *Thomas Aquinas: Approaches to Truth* (Dublin: Four Courts Press, 2002), 142–144.

⁵³ Ibid., 149.

⁵⁴ Ibid., 151.

⁵⁵ Ibid., 154.

⁵⁶ For example, Lonergan remarks, "It is not true that it is from sense that our cognitional activities derive their immediate relationship to real objects; that relationship is immediate in the intention of being; it is mediate in the data of sense . . . inasmuch as the intention of being makes use of data in promoting cognitional process to knowledge of being." "Cognitional Structure," 235–236. Lonergan also remarks, "We first reach the unconditioned, secondly we make a true judgment of existence, and only thirdly in and through the true judgment do we come to know actual and concrete existence." "*Insight*: Preface to a Discussion," in Crowe, *Collection*, 163. Both remarks flesh out Lonergan's claim about Aquinas' *De Veritate* I, 9c: "Rather, in this passage Aquinas subscribed, not obscurely, to the program of critical thought; to know truth we have to know ourselves and the nature of our knowledge, and the method to be employed is reflection." Bernard J. F. Lonergan, *Verbum: Word and Idea in Aquinas* (Notre Dame, IN: University of Notre Dame Press, 1970), 75. In his "How *A Priori* Is Lonergan?" *Proceedings of the American Catholic Philosophical Association* 79 (2005): 110–111, Samuel B. Condic disputes my previously published characterization of Lonergan's intention of being as a constitutive a priori. The notion of being cannot be a constitutive a priori because it determines "nothing in advance." As Lonergan is quoted, the notion of being leaves one free to be a materialist, empiricist, phenomenalist, or an idealist. Hence, Condic concludes, "What a particular being might be; indeed, what 'to be' might mean at all will be entirely and thoroughly a product of a reflective judgment on the 'given.'" While I agree with Condic's a posteriori epistemology, I must disagree that this is Lonergan. In reply, what Condic overlooks is that in the texts cited, Lonergan is not speaking absolutely about the intention of being but speaking only in a certain respect. Lonergan calls this respect "a second remove." Here the content of being is defined in terms of the totality of correct judgments, whatever those correct judgments may be—for example, realist, idealist, empiricist, or phenomenalist. For example, see the start of the paragraph in which Lonergan says, "The notion of being does not determine which position is correct." *Insight: A Study of Human Understanding* (New York: Longmans, 1965), 361. The qualification of "second remove" admits a first-order consideration of the notion of being. In this first-order consideration, being plays, as described above, a key role in determining what judgments are correct and so, in my opinion, is a constitutive a priori. Condic fails to realize this first-order consideration of being in Lonergan. For further consideration of texts expressing Lonergan's basic epistemology of attaining the "virtually unconditioned," see

John F. X. Knasas, "Why for Lonergan Knowing Cannot Consist in 'Taking a Look,'" *American Catholic Philosophical Quarterly* 78 (2004): 131–150.

Also, in "Aquinas: The Nature of Truth," *Continuum* 2 (1964): 70, Karl Rahner says, "In this way we also see what truth meant for St. Thomas in this degree of that self-consciousness which is always necessarily joined to true judgments. For man, truth is only in the judgment. The judgment supposes abstraction and self-consciousness. Both are possible only because of the transcendental *a priori* of spirit, which opens on the horizon of being as such. In this way a particular true judgment relative to concrete being is possible only in an implicit, though formal, judgment of being as such, and by means of that judgment, i.e., in a comprehension of being as such; and therefore, in the ultimate analysis, it is an implicit affirmation of pure being of God himself. *Omnes cognoscentes implicite cognoscunt Deum in quolibet cognitio.* Truth is only possible in the presence of being as such." Finally, Joseph Maréchal says, "Considered as a moment in the intellect's ascent towards the final possession of the absolute 'truth,' which is the spirit's 'good,' [affirmation] implicitly (*exercite*) projects the particular data in the perspective of this ultimate End, and by so doing objectivates them before the subject." In Joseph Donceel, *A Maréchal Reader* (New York: Herder and Herder, 1970), 152.

[57] On what I consider to be the anachronism here, see my *Being and Some Twentieth-Century Thomists*, 126–128.

[58] In his "Thomist or Relativist? MacIntyre's Interpretation of *adequatio intellectus et rei*," *Jacques Maritain and the Many Ways of Knowing* (Washington, DC: The Catholic University of America Press, 2002), 118–119, W. Matthews Grant argues that MacIntyre holds an internalist theory of justification in which rational justification is grounded in what is internal and introspectively accessible to the knower. In Grant's opinion, if MacIntyre is to escape relativism, MacIntyre must incorporate an externalist theory in which knowledge is constituted by certain states or processes that are external and not introspectively accessible to the knower. One feature of the externalism is that "justification is under the informing influence of reality, an influence to which we have no introspective access, but which accounts for the fact that systems of belief are not closed systems and that our activities of enquiry and justification—through which we come to know and to which we do have introspective access—yield truth, even if slowly and with much difficulty." Of course the question is why openness of systems should be interpreted as yielding truth in the Thomistic sense.

[59] MacIntyre, "Moral Relativism," 219.

[60] David Schindler, "Reorienting the Church on the Eve of the Millennium: John Paul II's 'New Evangelization,'" *Communio* 24 (1997), 751.

[61] Ibid., 754.

[62] Ibid., 755. Also, "Relative to the problem of the constitutional order of society, then, the pope's position clearly implies that an 'empty' or neutral or 'articles of peace' juridical order is not necessary to secure religious freedom for all citizens as a matter of principle." Ibid., 768–769.

[63] Ibid., 738.

[64] David L. Schindler, "God and the End of Intelligence: Knowledge as Relationship," *Communio* 26 (1999), 518.

[65] "As de Lubac says, 'the affirmation of the Infinite . . . , as implicit affirmation, [is] a constitutive condition of our apperception of particular objects.'" Ibid., 522. Schindler goes on to quote de Lubac to say that this affirmation "is a logical condition which preceded and

really constitutes the apperception of finite objects, then, certainly, we can neither deny it nor withdraw it without flagrant contradiction."

[66] Ibid., 526–527. Using the same ontology of knowledge, but as presented in Luigi Guissani's "religious sense," Schindler again argues against intolerance by arguing against integralism. See David Schindler, "'The Religious Sense' and American Culture," *Communio* 25 (1998), 690–691. Finally, another rendition of the argument against integralism, now called "confessionalism," can be found in David L. Schindler, *Heart of the World, Center of the Church: Communio Ecclesiology, Liberalism, and Liberation* (Grand Rapids, MI: Eerdmans, 1996), 82–88.

[67] Ibid., 529–534.

[68] Some doubt exists about whether de Lubac thought that the intellect's dynamism to the Infinite is in principle philosophically discernable. He says that this desire is so radically set in human nature that it remained hidden from the Gentiles. Only Christian revelation with its datum of the divine call lays bare man's desire for God. See *The Mystery of the Supernatural*, trans. by Rosemary Sheed (New York: Herder and Herder, 1967), 176–177; 274, "Certain depths of our nature can be opened only by the shock of revelation. Then, with a new clarity, deep calls upon deep." Ibid., 282. "But for us, unlike Cajetan, it is not the absence of any desire that is the reason for that ignorance: rather it is the depth of our desire." Ibid., 285. De Lubac admits a "sign" of the desire. The sign is the amplitude of the human intellect (ibid., 22). But only Christian revelation assures that the sign is correctly interpreted: "But in order to interpret that sign so well, to discern so clearly in it the desire to see the first cause in his very essence, it was surely necessary for St. Thomas to be at least 'oriented' by his faith." Ibid., 284. My question concerns the kind of "necessity" mentioned here. Specifically, is it necessary in fact or necessary in principle?

[69] Henri de Lubac, *The Discovery of God* (New York: P. J. Kennedy & Sons, 1960), 89.

[70] It is interesting to note that de Lubac's connection with Maréchal's project to get Thomistic conclusions for Kant's transcendental philosophy means that Schindler's ontology of knowledge is distinctly modern. Hence, Rowland's trumpeting of Schindler should compromise her wishes to be a "postmodern" Augustinian Thomist.

[71] For the details of this phenomenology, see my *Being and Some Twentieth-Century Thomists* (New York: Fordham University Press, 2003), chs. 3 and 4; also Joseph Owens, *Cognition: An Epistemological Inquiry* (Houston: Center for Thomistic Studies, 1992), ch. 2.

[72] For example, Knasas, *Being and Some Twentieth-Century Thomists*, ch. 9, sec. 2.

[73] Ibid., ch. 9, secs. 5 and 6. Also, my "The Liberationist Critique of Maritain's New Christendom" *The Thomist* 52 (1988), 247–268, explains how Maritain's "distinction of temporal and spiritual planes" model need not employ a "closed" view of the temporal characteristic of Cajetan.

[74] On the nature of the qualifications to the *ratio entis* to understand how the Thomistic metaphysician's proof of God's existence provides at least a confused and imperfect knowledge of the divine quiddity, see my *Being and Some Twentieth-Century Thomists*, ch. 7, secs. 6 and 7.

VII

SUMMARY

Ideas from Aquinas solve the philosophical problem of truth and tolerance. The problem is as follows. On the one hand, how can you believe that you philosophically possess the truth and also be tolerant of others? On the other hand, maintaining that no truth exists also invites intolerance. The solution is to disagree with the first part. Among the various ethics in the history of philosophy, Aquinas' natural law ethics best accommodates tolerance. *Tolerance* means something stronger than mutual indifference. Tolerance is nonapproval but acceptance of difference within a context of mutual goodwill and brotherly love. In chapter II, I explained that, in Aquinas' philosophical analyses, grounds exist to characterize the human as an intellector of being. Since being is also the good, I concluded that each human stands forth as a particularly intense presentation of the good and obviously should be treated with respect and solicitude.

As lofty as the intellector of being sounds, it is congruent with the facts of human behavior. Chapter II concluded by explaining how passions and our default position of freedom unfortunately afford prompts for the intellector of being to be disrespectful. Moreover, chapter III argued that since the notion of being is such an automatic abstraction from the realities of sense experience, it can go unnoticed in our conscious life, though conscious effects of its presence exist. These conscious effects include some inchoate sense of human dignity, the impropriety of contradiction, freedom, and even an ordinary knowledge of God. The result is that, despite ourselves, we are all intellectors of being, and a clever philosopher stands a chance of leading us to appreciate our nature. Though Aquinas is no Platonist who holds that knowledge is virtue, Aquinas does hold that knowledge has an effect in morals. Hence, the number of angels that remained firm is greater than the number who fell.

In chapter IV, I explained how this understanding of the human leads to a social philosophy in which disagreements are addressed on an intellectual level. Intellect must address intellect, diamond must cut

147

diamond. Furthermore, Aquinas' approach accommodates tolerance by preparing us to acknowledge that the human good is analogously realized. Though there are definite ways of being bad, this moral fact places no straightjacket on the innumerable definite ways for being good. Each person's fidelity to the intuition of being in oneself and others will lead each person to be good in the manner particular to one's time and place. Finally, the analogous character of being, understood as the good, enables a Thomist to make some reply to Heidegger's call for an authentic existence in which we create something unique to ourselves.

Chapter V extended Aquinas' thinking into political philosophy. Aquinas' ideas limit the state to the protection of the common good from the most serious actions against the common good. The state cannot solve philosophical problems. Though the state would welcome a philosophical defense of tolerance, the state does not require it in order to espouse tolerance. The history of the twentieth century has taught us that truth. Yet the state is aware that certain philosophies cannot accommodate this truth. It allows these philosophies to suffer critical scrutiny in the marketplace of ideas and restricts itself to defending tolerance from only the most grievous practical implications of these philosophies. In sum, Aquinas' view of the state is one in which the state encourages its citizens to discover a way to live as brothers. Aquinas' texts on heretics and Jews are congruent with tolerance.

Finally, Aquinas helps one to understand how a country can westernize without losing its cultural identity. Becoming Western by becoming democratic (and hence, tolerant) does not mean diminishing one's identity, as some skeptic proponents of tolerance say. To the contrary, the only viable philosophical way to become tolerant is to be in some way faithful to ourselves as intellectors of being. That fidelity not only generates a strong positive sense of tolerance, but it also produces a distinctive way of life among those involved. Morality is the basis for cultural identity. Just as the call to holiness in Catholicism led to an unforeseeable array of saintly identities that were not mutually destructive, so too, the call for respect and solicitude of the intellector of being will do the same.

Far from being something new and yet to be tried, morality has been the basis of culture. Dawson's reflections on culture show that the religious impulse has always been the operative factor in the birth and development of cultures. This view of culture means that something good exists in every culture. The challenge is to engage that culture and to discover the good elements. Aquinas' philosophical psychology of the intellector of being is, in my opinion, an indispensable hermeneutical tool for cultural analysis.

Aquinas' philosophical insights amply repay the effort needed to attain them. Aquinas' natural law ethics not only accommodates tolerance but also provides tolerance with a high benchmark. Without doubt, few will possess the talents necessary to actualize tolerance in the line of Aquinas. Though ad hominem dismissals remain philosophically inappropriate, we dread the thought that our lives will always be an embarrassment to our principles. Hopefully, we have known some individuals who have come close to the ideal. Jacques Maritain occurs to my mind. Appearing in the pages of Jean-Luc Barré's recent biography[1] is a Thomist devoted in deep love to his fellow man—especially the artists, intellectuals, and the poor. Repeatedly, Barré quotes the initial reactions of those of other persuasions to Maritain. They all mention Maritain's gentleness, his ability to listen, and his uncanny ability to perceive the essence of a discussion—in short, his friendship. One cannot read these reactions without measuring one's life to Maritain's.

In conclusion, if one understands tolerance in the context of fraternity to be fundamental to the common good of a democratic society, then being tolerant need not mean neutering oneself culturally by becoming secular and skeptical. That latter defense of tolerance has exhausted itself and is the biggest problem in "selling liberty" to other nations of the world. To many people, from the secular perspective, liberty appears to mean license. And so when others hear an American say the word *liberty*, what comes to mind is the Hollywood lifestyle. I have tried to point out that one better preserves tolerance/fraternity by delineating ideas from the ethical thought of Thomas Aquinas. There are more and better *apologiae* for democratic government than the philosophical deconstructions so popularized in Western circles.

Note:

[1] Jean-Luc Barré, *Jacques and Raïssa Maritain: Beggars for Heaven*. Trans. by Bernard E. Doering (Notre Dame, IN: University of Notre Dame Press, 2005).

BIBLIOGRAPHY

Anderson, Benedict. *Imagined Communities: Reflections on the Origin and Spread of Nationalism*. London: Verso, 1991.

Anderson, James. *The Bond of Being: An Essay on Analogy and Existence*. New York: Greenwood Press, 1969.

Aquinas, St. Thomas. *In Duodecim Libros Metaphysicorum Aristotelis Expositio*. Eds. M. R. Cathala and Raymundus M. Spiazzi. Turin and Rome: Marietti, 1950.

———. *Liber de Veritate Catholicae Fidei contra Errores Infidelium seu "Summa Contra Gentiles."* Eds. Ceslaus Pera, Petrus Marc, Petrus Caramello. Turin and Rome: Marietti, 1961.

———. *Quaestiones Disputatae de Veritate*. Ed. by Raymundus Spiazzi. In *Quaestiones Disputatae*, I. Turin and Rome: Marietti, 1964.

———. *Summa Theologiae*. Ed. Ottawa Institute of Mediaeval Studies. Ottawa: Collège Dominicain d'Ottawa, 1941.

Aristotle. *Metaphysics*. Ed. Richard McKeon. *The Basic Works of Aristotle*. New York: Random House, 1970.

Augustine, St. *De Libero Arbitrio*. Ed., in *Corpus Christianorum, Series Latina* (Turnholti: Typographi Brepols Editores Pontificii, 1970), XXIX.

Barré, Jean-Luc. *Jacques and Raïssa Maritain: Beggars for Heaven*. Trans. Bernard E. Doering. Notre Dame, IN: University of Notre Dame Press, 2005.

Bernstein, Richard J. "Metaphysics, Critique, and Utopia." *The Review of Metaphysics* 42 (1988): 255–274.

Boguslawski, Steven. *Thomas Aquinas on the Jews*. New York: Paulist Press, 2008.

Bonaventure, St. *Itinerarium Mentis in Deum*. Trans. and commentary by Philotheus Boehner. Saint Bonaventure, NY: The Franciscan Institute, Saint Bonaventure University, 1956.

Bourke, Vernon J. Trans. With introduction and notes of St. Thomas Aquinas' *Summa Contra Gentiles*, vol. 3. Notre Dame, IN: University of Notre Dame Press, 1975.

Brock, Werner. Ed. *Martin Heidegger: Existence and Being*. Chicago, IL: Henry Regnery, 1968.

Burrell, David C. "Faith, Culture, and Reason: Analogous Language and Truth." *Proceedings of the American Catholic Philosophical Association* 77 (2003): 1–11.

Čiubrinskas Vytis, "Identity and the Revival of Tradition in Lithuania: An Insider's View." *Folk* 42 (2000): 19–40.

Condic, Samuel B. "How *A Priori* Is Lonergan?" *Proceedings of the American Catholic Philosophical Association* 79 (2005): 103–116.

Copleston, Frederick. *A History of Philosophy, Mediaeval Philosophy*, vol. 2, pt. 1. Garden City, NY: Image Books, 1962.

Crowe, F. E., Ed. *Collection: Papers by Bernard Lonergan, S.J.* New York: Herder & Herder, 1967.

Dawson, Christopher. *Progress and Religion: An Historical Enquiry*. Washington, DC: The Catholic University of America Press, 2001.

———. *Religion and Culture*. New York: Sheed & Ward, 1948.

De Lubac, Henri. *The Discovery of God*. New York: P. J. Kennedy & Sons, 1960.

————. *The Mystery of the Supernatural*. Trans. Rosemary Sheed. New York: Herder & Herder, 1967.

Dewey, John. *Reconstruction in Philosophy*. Boston: Beacon Press, 1968.

Diogenes Laertius. *Lives of the Philosophers*. Trans. and ed. A. Robert Caponigii. Chicago, IL: Henry Regnery, 1969.

Donceel, Joseph. *A Maréchal Reader*. New York: Herder & Herder, 1970.

Dupré, Louis. *Metaphysics and Culture*. Milwaukee, WI: Marquette University Press, 1994.

Gilson, Etienne. *The Unity of Philosophical Experience*. New York: Charles Scribner's Sons, 1937.

Heidegger, Martin. *The Basic Problems of Phenomenology*. Trans. Albert Hofstadter. Bloomington: Indiana University Press, 1988.

————. *Being and Time*. Trans. John Macquarie and Edward Robinson. New York: Harper & Row, 1962.

————. "Hölderlin and the Essence of Poetry." In Werner Brock, ed., *Martin Heidegger: Existence and Being*.

————. *Introduction to Metaphysics*. Trans. Ralph Manheim. New Haven, CT: Yale University Press, 1977.

————. *Letter on Humanism*. In David Farrell Krell, ed., *Martin Heidegger: Basic Writings*.

Hood, John Y. B. *Aquinas and the Jews*. Philadelphia: University of Pennsylvania Press, 1995.

Hume David, *A Treatise of Human Nature*. T. H. Green and T. H. Grose, eds., *David Hume: The Philosophical Works*. Darmstadt: Scientia Verlag Aalen, 1964.

Kant, Immanuel. *Groundwork of the Metaphysics of Morals*. Trans. Mary Gregor. Cambridge: Cambridge University Press, 1998.

Kirn, Arthur G., ed. *G. B. Phelan: Selected Papers.* Toronto: Pontifical Institute of Mediaeval Studies, 1967.

Klubertanz, George P. *St. Thomas on Analogy.* Chicago, IL: Loyola University Press, 1960.

Knasas, John F. X. *Being and Some Twentieth-Century Thomists.* New York: Fordham University Press, 2003.

————. "Incommensurability and Aquinas' Metaphysics." *Proceedings of the American Catholic Philosophical Association* 65 (1991): 179–190.

————. "The Liberationist Critique of Maritain's New Christendom." *The Thomist* 52 (1988): 247–268.

————. "Thomistic Reflections on Stasys Šalkauskis' Philosophy of Culture." *Soter* (Journal of the Faculty of Theology, Vytautas Magnus University, Kaunas, Lithuania) 29 (2009): 7–16.

————. "Why for Lonergan Knowing Cannot Consist in 'Taking a Look.'" *American Catholic Philosophical Quarterly* 78 (2004): 131–150.

Knight, Kelvin. Ed. *The MacIntyre Reader.* Notre Dame, IN: University of Notre Dame Press, 1998.

Krell, David Farrell. Ed. *Martin Heidegger: Basic Writings.* New York: Harper & Row, 1977.

Locke, John. *A Letter Concerning Toleration.* Ed., Mario Montnori. The Hague: Martinus Nijhoff, 1963.

Lonergan, Bernard J. F. "Cognitional Structure." In F. E. Crowe, ed., *Collection: Papers by Bernard Lonergan, S.J.*

————. "Insight: Preface to a Discussion." In F. E. Crowe, ed., *Collection: Papers by Bernard Lonergan, S.J.*

————. *Insight: A Study of Human Understanding*. New York: Longmans, 1965.

————. *Verbum: Word and Idea in Aquinas*. Notre Dame, IN: University of Notre Dame Press, 1970.

Lowery, Atherton. "The Metaphysics of Culture: Its Being, Its Life, and Its Death." *Proceedings of the American Catholic Philosophical Association* 77 (2003): 247–258.

MacIntyre, Alasdair. *First Principles, Final Ends, and Contemporary Philosophical Issues*. Milwaukee, WI: Marquette University Press, 1990.

————. "Moral Relativism, Truth and Justification." In Kelvin Knight, ed., *The MacIntyre Reader*.

————. *Three Rival Versions of Moral Enquiry*. Notre Dame, IN: University of Notre Dame Press, 1990.

————. "Truth as a Good: A Reflection on *Fides et Ratio*." In James McEvoy and Michael Dunne, eds., *Thomas Aquinas: Approaches to Truth*.

Maritain, Jacques. *Art and Scholasticism*. London: Sheed & Ward, 1946.

————. *Integral Humanism: Temporal and Spiritual Problems of a New Christendom*. Notre Dame, IN: University of Notre Dame Press, 1973.

————. "The Natural Mystical Experience and the Void," in his *Ransoming the Time*. New York: Gordian Press, 1972.

————. *The Sin of the Angel*. Westminster, MD: Newman Press, 1959.

Maurer, Armand A., trans. with introduction and notes on St. Thomas Aquinas, *On Being and Essence*. Toronto: Pontifical Institute of Mediaeval Studies, 1968.

————. *Medieval Philosophy*. New York: Random House, 1965.

Maxwell, Michael P. "A Dialectical Encounter between MacIntyre and Lonergan on the Thomistic Understanding of Rationality." *International Philosophical Quarterly* 33 (1993): 385–400.

McEvoy, James. "The Other as Oneself: Friendship and Love in the Thought of St. Thomas Aquinas." In James McEvoy and Michael Dunne, eds., *Thomas Aquinas: Approaches to Truth.*

————, and Michael Dunne, eds. *Thomas Aquinas: Approaches to Truth.* Dublin: Four Courts Press, 2002.

McKeon, Richard. Ed. *The Basic Works of Aristotle*. New York: Random House, 1970.

Mill, John Stuart. *Utilitarianism*. Indianapolis, IN: Bobbs-Merrill, 1957.

Newman, John Henry Cardinal. *The Idea of a University*. Ed. Martin J. Svaglic. Notre Dame, IN: University of Notre Dame Press, 1982.

O'Connor, William R. *The Eternal Quest: The Teaching of St. Thomas Aquinas on the Natural Desire for God*. New York: Longmans, Green, 1947.

Owens, Joseph. "Analogy as a Thomistic Approach to Being." *Mediaeval Studies* 24 (1962): 303–322.

————. *The Doctrine of Being in the Aristotelian Metaphysics*. Toronto: Pontifical Institute of Mediaeval Studies, 1963.

————. *An Elementary Christian Metaphysics*. Houston, TX: Center for Thomistic Studies, 1985.

Pegis, Anton C. Ed. *The Basic Writings of St. Thomas Aquinas*. New York: Random House, 1945.

————. Trans. with introduction and notes on St. Thomas Aquinas, *Summa Contra Gentiles*, vol. 1. Notre Dame, IN: University of Notre Dame Press, 1975.

Phelan, Gerald B. "St. Thomas and Analogy." Pp. 95–122. In Arthur G. Kirn, ed., *G. B. Phelan: Selected Papers*. Toronto: Pontifical Institute of Mediaeval Studies, 1967.

Pieper, Josef. *Leisure: The Basis of Culture*. New York: The New American Library of World Literature, 1963.

Rahner, Karl. "Aquinas: The Nature of Truth." *Continuum* 2 (1964): 60–72.

Ratzinger, Joseph Cardinal. *Truth and Tolerance: Christian Belief and World Religions*. Trans. Henry Taylor. San Francisco: Ignatius Press, 2003.

Rawls, John. *Political Liberalism*. New York: Columbia University Press, 1993.

———. *A Theory of Justice*. Cambridge, MA: Harvard University Press, 1971.

Rorty, Richard. *Contingency, Irony, and Solidarity*. Cambridge: Cambridge University Press, 1989.

———. "Cosmopolitanism without Emancipation: A Response to Jean-François Lyotard." In Rorty, *Objectivity, Relativism, and Truth*, 211–222.

———. "Feminism and Pragmatism." In Rorty, *Truth and Progress*, 202–227.

———. "Habermas, Derrida, and Philosophy." In Rorty, *Truth and Progress*, 307–326.

———. "Human Rights, Rationality, and Sentimentality." In Rorty, *Truth and Progress*, 167–185.

———. *Objectivity, Relativism, and Truth*. Cambridge: Cambridge University Press, 1991.

————. "On Ethnocentrism: A Reply to Clifford Geertz." In Rorty, *Objectivity, Relativism, and Truth*, 203–210.

————. *Philosophy and the Mirror of Nature*. Princeton, NJ: Princeton University Press, 1980.

————. "The Priority of Democracy to Philosophy." In Rorty, *Objectivity, Relativism, and Truth*, 175–196.

————. "Postmodernist Bourgeois Liberalism." In Rorty, *Objectivity, Relativism, and Truth*, 197–202.

————. *Truth and Progress: Philosophical Papers, Volume 3*. Cambridge: Cambridge University Press, 1998.

Rowland, Tracey. *Culture and the Thomist Tradition after Vatican II*. London: Routledge, 2003.

Russman, Thomas A. *A Prospectus for the Triumph of Realism*. Macon, GA: Mercer University Press, 1987.

Schindler, David L. "God and the End of Intelligence: Knowledge as Relationship." *Communio* 26 (1999): 510–540.

————. *Heart of the World, Center of the Church: Communion Ecclesiology, Liberalism, and Liberation*. Grand Rapids, MI: Eerdmans, 1996.

————. "The 'Religious Sense' and American Culture." *Communio* 25 (1998): 679–699.

————. "Reorienting the Church on the Eve of the Millennium: John Paul II's 'New Evangelization.'" *Communio* 24 (1997): 728–779.

Schmidt, Robert W. Trans. of St. Thomas Aquinas, *The Disputed Questions on Truth*, vol. 3. Chicago, IL: Henry Regnery, 1954.

Shirer, William L. *The Rise and Fall of the Third Reich*. New York: Simon & Schuster, 1960.

Sartre, Jean-Paul. *Existentialism and Humanism*. Trans. Philip Mairet. London: Methuen, 1948.

Tereškinas, Arturas. "Between Soup and Soap: Iconic Nationality, Mass Media and Pop Culture in Contemporary Lithuania." *Lituanus* 46 (2000): 14–47.

UNESCO. "Declaration of Principles on Tolerance." At http://portal.unesco.org/en/ev.php-URL_ID=13175&URL_DO=DO_TOPIC& URL_SECTION=201.html.

Walzer, Michael. *On Toleration*. New Haven, CT: Yale University Press, 1997.

Wippel, John, and Alan Wolter. *Medieval Philosophy from St. Augustine to Nicholas of Cusa*. New York: Free Press, 1969.

INDEX

A

absolute, tendency toward, 52
absolutely infinite, 15
abstraction, 52–53, 116, 129
actus essendi (the act of being), 36
adultery, 50
Aeschylus, 86
Aeterni patris (Leo XIII), 3
altruism, 66
American Indians, 85–86, 87, 88, 91
Americanization, 109, 112, 149
analogons, 15, 18–19, 49–51, 142 n 44
Anderson, Benedict, 109
Anderson, James, 27 n 3
angels, 26, 48, 147
Anscombe, Elizabeth, 130
Anselm, 15
Aquinas, Thomas
        on human dignity, 13–14
        intellectual discourses by, 3
        naivety, charge of, 2
        and natural truths, 9–10
Aquinas and the Jews (Hood), 95–100
Aristotle, 18, 39, 42 n 17, 46, 59 n 6,
        131, 138
art, 57–58
articulation and self-evidency, 39–40
assimilation and change in culture, 114
atheism, 107–108
Atman (Self), 120–121
Augustine, 16–17, 104 n 73, 110, 127–
        128
Augustinian Thomism, 126–129
automatic abstraction, 32
autonomy of will, 68–71, 90
awareness and sense, 32

B

Bacon, Francis, 85
baptizing of Jewish children, 97
Barré, Jean-Luc, 149
Basic Problems of Phenomenology, The
        (Heidegger), 54, 55, 56–57
beatitude, 67
being. *See ratio entis*
Being and Nothingness (Sartre), 60 n 21
Being and Time (Heidegger), 59
Belnap, Nuel, Jr., 130
Bernstein, Richard J., 10 n 5
Boguslawski, Steven, 105 n 80
Bonaventure, 17, 111
Bono, 64
Bosnian genocide, 86
Buddhism, 120–121
Burrell, David B., 140 n 6

C

Cajetan, 102 n 50, 137, 145
Camp, Joseph, Jr., 130
Caputo, John, 59
Catholic philosophers, bias against, 111
Catholicism
        and cultural pluralism, 110–111
        and meaning of humanity, 133
        in political liberalism, 80–81
causality, 38, 129, 137–138
change and assimilation in culture, 114
children, beliefs of, 81, 97
Christ
        as communication of creator, 138
        and Judaism, 95–97
        and meaning of humanity, 133
Christian confessional state, 133–134